FOSTER CARE

FOSTER CARE

How to Fix This Corrupted System

Janet Solander

iUniverse LLC
Bloomington

FOSTER CARE
How to Fix This Corrupted System

iUniverse books may be ordered through booksellers or by contacting:

iUniverse LLC
1663 Liberty Drive
Bloomington, IN 47403
www.iuniverse.com
1-800-Authors (1-800-288-4677)

ISBN: 978-1-4917-1108-8 (sc)
ISBN: 978-1-4917-1107-1 (hc)
ISBN: 978-1-4917-1106-4 (e)

Library of Congress Control Number: 2013918817

Printed in the United States of America.

iUniverse rev. date: 11/15/2013

This book is dedicated to all those children who tragically lost their lives because of the failures of those charged with protecting and caring for them. It is also dedicated to the memory of my mother, Robbie Jean, through whose guidance I was able to raise four beautiful daughters—Tara, Kimberlee, Dominique, and Danielle—who have blessed me with five grandchildren so far. Also for my wonderful husband, Dwight, without whose support this book would not be possible. Lastly, to our three adopted daughters—Ava, Amaya, and Anastasia—as well as all the children we have fostered and cared for. It is my hope that the contents of this book will save even more lives of foster and adopted children throughout the United States. A further goal is to help more children be safely and successfully adopted through the foster-care system.

Contents

Introduction

Imagine you are a child living in what may not be the most desirable conditions. One day there is a knock on the door. It is the police, there to arrest Mommy and Daddy, and a Child Protective Services (CPS) worker to take you away with him or her. You have about fifteen minutes to gather what clothes and toys you can and throw them in a trash bag, and away you go.

The next thing you know, you're at a holding station. A few hours after that, you are brought to a strange home and told this is where you are going to stay until Mommy and Daddy get better. With any luck, you will have been placed in a good home where the foster parents are caring for you out of love and kindness and are truly concerned for your welfare. If not, your situation may have just gotten worse.

There are many reasons why children are taken out of their home by CPS, and it can be very traumatic. Whatever the reason behind it, as a child you now find yourself with strange people in a strange home, and your first question is going to be "Why?"

At this point, the new foster parent must have a good understanding of the emotions that are overwhelming the child. The child does not know what has just happened, why it happened, or how long it is going to continue. There is mostly confusion at first, and then questions. In many cases, there may be misplaced anger toward the new home. Many children become so overwhelmed that they do not know how to deal with their emotions.

Often, children who wind up in foster care have not had a typical upbringing and may have been pretty much fending for themselves most of their lives. They do not trust anyone, and they will usually shut down. There is no outlet for these children to adjust to the feelings they are experiencing and be reassured that it is not their fault. Can you blame them for acting out?

The easiest and most defiant way for a child to vent is by urinating or defecating in his or her pants, on the bed, or on another object. We have witnessed this behavior many times with foster children. If the foster parents do not understand that this is a behavior that could potentially surface and have not been trained to deal with it, they may not react appropriately. It is especially maddening for foster parents who have children of their own and never had to go through anything remotely similar with their own kids.

This is where the rage could start for foster parents. They are not expecting this, and they have never seen such behavior. They think the foster kids are disrespecting them intentionally, which is not at all the case. Many foster parents do not stop to realize or try to understand what is going on in a child's mind. This needs to be explained to prospective foster parents during training classes and then repeated over and over.

Rage can all too easily shift into abuse of the child. Remember, these are children who have never been taught the proper way to deal with emotions. Now they are being abused again in a different setting that they were promised would be safe and secure. Soon this begins to escalate, with the kids acting out now against the new home as well as trying to tackle the original feelings they have not been able to cope with. Ultimately, there is a breaking point, and something bad happens to the child and then to the foster parent.

This outcome can be prevented. The cycle can be broken. It starts with proper training for foster parents to help them manage this type of irrational behavior—a more intense form of training than is currently available. In many cases where abuse occurs, foster parents have been blindsided by behavioral issues they were never prepared for. Training classes tend to sugarcoat the reality of how foster children behave and how many of them exhibit extreme behaviors.

Foster parents have the option of returning a placement if it does not work out, and while this is certainly preferable to an abusive situation, it results in foster children shifting from one home to the next to the next, compounding the emotional damage and educating the children in how to work the system. They realize that foster parents have very limited options for disciplinary action, and they act out knowing there is nothing the foster parents can do without incurring a visit from their caseworker.

From personal experience, I can say that most children in the system for the first time or who have been in the system for a short period of time will have minimal behavior issues. Younger children also do not tend to act out or have as bad of a coping issue as older children do, as they are too young to really understand the full magnitude of what is going on. It is the older children who have been in a biological home with no guidance and have come to expect that they can do whatever they want who will cause the most problems. Most of these children know very well how to manipulate the system and will not respect any authority, or will report you to their caseworker with false allegations.

I have experienced this firsthand. The children figure that if they report you, they will be taken out of your home and placed with someone else they can also manipulate to get away with anything they want. This cycle will continue until they term out of the system, and then they will have a serious reality check. Unfortunately, criminal activity is usually the result, with prison becoming their next home.

Foster care starts out as a way to rescue children from a bad situation, but the system fails these vulnerable young victims again and again, and it fails the people trying to make a better life for them. The system in Nevada, where my husband and I live, is overloaded with foster children, and the need to place them is prioritized over the need to find the right home. In talking with foster parents here, we have met many who, although theirs is a low-maintenance foster home, have received placements requiring a higher level of care. There is no full disclosure of mental-health issues and other special needs, leaving foster parents unequipped to provide needed help. The workers in the system are overwhelmed, with caseloads far too great to provide effective and safe servicing of all active cases. This has been our own experience through many foster placements, and other foster parents we speak with report the same issues.

Jorge and Carmen Barahona, Shameeka Davis, and Renée Bowman—all former foster parents—are examples of the worst that can happen as a result of the system's shortcomings. Jorge and Carmen are currently in custody awaiting trial, while Shameeka and Renée are serving time in prison for murdering the foster/adopted children in their care. In each of these cases, CPS failed the victims. These are not isolated incidents. The exact numbers of victimized children is not known, as there are many cases that go unreported, are reported with a different reason, or are reported as missing or runaways. Unfortunately, most of these victims of abuse go unnoticed until it is too late.

In this book, you will read about our experiences with the foster-care system, as well as the experiences we had adopting our three daughters out of foster care in Clark County, Nevada. You will see how the system is designed for the benefit of the natural parents at the expense of the children who have been placed in foster care because of the parents' actions and inability to care for them for one reason or another—usually drug abuse, physical abuse, or neglect. You will read about the many failings and shortcomings in the current system and the many ways we feel it could be changed for the benefit of the children who are placed in this system.

While my husband and I both feel that we were deceived in regard to full disclosure on the true history of the children we foster-parented and then adopted, and that the system was not forthcoming about all the issues we could expect, that still is no reason to neglect, abuse, or murder the children. We both feel that it was divine intervention on behalf of these children that they were placed with us. That may sound conceited, but we have always felt that the behaviors these children have displayed could otherwise have resulted in multiple failed adoption attempts until they termed out of the system, or they would have been placed in a family that would not have the tolerance and patience we do and would have ended up as a statistic.

We have been foster parents for close to four years as of the beginning of 2013, and we have fostered over twenty children in that time, most of them long-term (more than six months). We adopted our three girls after fostering them. We are also active in advocating for reform in the way CPS cases are handled and the way the court system ignores federal statutes and considers the rights of the biological parents over the welfare of the children in too many cases.

While this book describes our experiences with the agencies in Clark County, after speaking with foster parents here and in other areas of the United States, I have found that the situation is no different anywhere else. My husband's job requires extensive travel throughout the United States and has presented him with multiple opportunities to speak with people on this issue. There is overwhelming dissatisfaction with the way foster and adoptive parents are treated, and with the fact that, in many cases, foster parents are given no consideration at all.

The most disturbing theme that comes up again and again in these conversations is the lack of concern for the children and the overwhelming inclination of family judges to reunify families at all costs. When foster parents take care of these children, they are with the children twenty-four hours a day, seven days a week. The judges in these cases only see the parents for an average of half an hour every two months or so for a hearing on the progress of the case. The unfortunate circumstance is that these hearings do not involve the children at all. There is never even a mention of them, other than the parents begging to get their children back.

This has led to a steady decline in the number of available foster homes while at the same time the need for homes increases every day. This situation has caused foster-care agencies to become overworked, with extremely high caseloads for the workers. It's also caused many guidelines, rules, and statutes to be bent at both the agency and the courtroom level, to get kids into homes regardless of whether the placement is appropriate or the foster parents are prepared to provide the proper care.

Trust me when I say it is not easy living with the disorders and bizarre behaviors these children express, but after considerable research and questioning others about these issues, we have been able to narrow down the underlying causes. By sharing our personal experiences and the conclusions we have drawn because of them, I hope to help other parents become better informed about potential issues and learn how to do their own research. Though the system must be reformed, there is much that foster and adoptive parents can do to help themselves in the meantime.

Chapter 1

A Brief History of Foster Homes

Foster care in the United States has been around since the early part of the twentieth century. Early on, most of the children needing this type of care because of family issues of one type or another were placed in orphanages, the only viable option at that time. By the year 1910, there were over a thousand orphanages. However, by the early 1960s, there were more children in family foster care than there were in "institutions," which was the name commonly used for orphanages back then. This substantial increase in the availability of foster homes was due mainly to federal funding becoming available for foster care. This funding was made available when Aid to Families with Dependent Children (formerly Aid to Dependent Children) was enacted by the Social Security Act of 1935.

Many of the laws and regulations regarding foster care are more strictly enforced and monitored today than they were at the time they were enacted. Birth parents have more rights today than they did years ago. Today, if your children are in foster care, you still can make many decisions for them. Foster parents must have your permission to get the children's hair cut or to give them multivitamins. If a child's health is at risk and a surgical procedure is recommended, a court order may be needed if birth parents refuse to sign the medical consent forms. In Clark County, birth parents have more leniency during visits—for example, they would have to miss three visits in a row before their visits were suspended temporarily, and from our experience, sometimes they get a break even after that, because the goal is to work toward reunification at whatever the cost. Ultimately, there is more leniency today than there was years ago in regard to the part birth parents play in their children's lives while they are in foster care.

It is difficult to determine whether there was more or less abuse and fewer homicides in the early days of foster care compared to today because people stayed out of each other's business and pretty much kept to themselves. There were many differences in the attitudes and the general state of the country in those days compared to today, regarding both the care of children and the overall feeling of obligation to help one's neighbor. Because of this attitude in the country, in the early days of home care, children were placed in boarding homes paid for by agencies to the families that cared for them; however, many foster parents became involved in foster care for free labor called working homes, where mainly older children earned their keep by working on farms or with businesses—as opposed to many today who see it as an opportunity for financial gain. Although these working homes, commonly known as free homes, were quite rare, many of the children were never legally adopted.

When we took our initial training, there were several stories told about foster parents who took in placements that did not work out. When they gave the children back, they asked for some immediate replacements because the house payment was due. In our orientation, we were told of a foster family that needed to have a minimum of six foster children in their home at all times, because they needed to maintain their mortgage payment. These people were really serious! I get asked all the time about how nice it must be to get the extra money in and have to do nothing for it. This is just total ignorance of what is involved in caring for these children.

Our current foster children's mental-health counselors as well as several caseworkers we have worked with have commended my husband and me, saying they wish all foster parents were like us. They tell us that there are some foster parents who are in it for the money, and they can clearly tell that we aren't. Recently, when we took two of our foster kids to their scheduled dental surgery, the medical staff repeatedly thanked us for caring enough to be foster parents. One of the nurses even gave us a hug! The dental surgeon knew me very well, as he has performed dental surgery on at least one of each sibling group of children we have fostered in our four years as foster parents.

When we look at the way many children are dressed at foster events, it is very obvious that their foster parents are doing the bare minimum to care for them. I cannot remember a placement we have taken yet where we did not have to spend at least $500 each on clothes and toiletries the first day we took them. We are always complimented on how well our foster children look. We also know that the stipend that we receive barely if at all covers the expenses of fostering a child. The bottom line is that there is no money to be made as foster parents if the children are being taken care of properly.

An analogy could be drawn to a welfare program for financially stable people. The only difference would be that the stipend received requires some work to be performed, unlike welfare, which is more like a handout with no accountability. In the case of foster care, the accountability is to the ones who are supposed to be cared for—the children—and the idea that the standard of care is the bare minimum to keep the child alive. In some cases, as will be seen, even this standard is not being met. Some foster parents with strictly financial motives only see the children in their care as a paycheck and a mortgage payment. It is for this reason that many rules have been put in place to regulate foster homes and foster care in general, and that more emphasis has been placed on enforcing those rules.

Unfortunately, family-service departments in every county across the United States have a shortage of caseworkers (family-services specialists), making that enforcement difficult. Reports on these tragedies have a recurring theme: caseworkers did not visit the children when they should have, if at all. In many cases, this is because a relative was caring for the children and caseworkers did not feel the need to supervise closely. Such was the case with Shameeka Davis. The other issue that is brought to light is that the caseload is so high that the caseworker did not have the time to visit on the schedule that should have been followed. This has been seen as a factor in many cases when a child was murdered while in foster care.

The most recent monthly home visit from our foster children's caseworker was so rushed, she only saw the three older children and never asked to see the baby, who was sleeping soundly in one of our upstairs rooms. If something had happened to that baby, the caseworker would have never figured it out until the next monthly visit, because at that time visits with family members had been temporarily suspended. This is a tragic scenario that is disturbing to say the least.

We are currently licensed as a low-maintenance foster home with a license obtained through the county, and although we have forty hours of therapeutic-foster-care training, we are not yet licensed as a therapeutic foster home. Nevertheless, every child we have fostered—including the three we adopted—has had special needs related to mental and physical impairments. These placements were obviously made because of the lack of therapeutic foster homes available, as well as family-service specialists with larger-than-normal caseloads and more clients than they can accommodate in a fifty-hour week. Children with severe behavioral issues or disabilities are placed in any foster home available, which usually ends up being a nontherapeutic foster home. Placing these children in foster homes that do not have the capability to manage such behaviors is in the best interest of neither the child nor the foster family.

When family-service specialists are not able to effectively oversee their caseload, shortcuts are taken to try to satisfy reporting requirements. This results in short and ineffective visits—and in some cases, no visits at all. That is how these homes where abuse takes place are slipping through the cracks. The workers are so overwhelmed that they have to give attention to the cases that are glaring and put the cases that appear to have no issues on the back burner.

There are ways to solve this problem while also reducing the caseload of the Department of Family Services and ultimately requiring fewer foster homes. A large foster-care center that can house 1,500 to 3,000 foster children—or even more, depending on the state, donations, and funding—could significantly reduce the number of poorly placed foster children. If nothing else, at least it could be an overflow center for hard-to-place foster children, such as large sibling groups, and potentially adoptable children. In this case, much of the manpower currently being utilized out in the field could be focused more toward the center. The monthly payments used to pay individual foster homes can go toward the center.

It makes you wonder where all the foster children who are not currently in foster homes reside right now. One such place here in Clark County is a holding facility called Child Haven. This is supposed to be at most an overnight to forty-eight-hour holding facility until a foster placement is found, but I personally know of several children who have been there for many weeks because no home could be found. Even though this is run by Department of Family Services, the care is the bare minimum, and the children are for the most part left to take care of themselves.

The shocking secret about such places—one that unfortunately cannot be officially verified—is the use of treatment facilities to house children who need behavioral help when there is no foster placement available for them. This can be justified in many ways, I suppose. In theory, these children may be getting the help they need. The issue is that if there is no placement for them, they continue to receive "help" until Medicaid will not pay for any more services, which may mean quite a long stay.

This may sound like an extreme allegation. Short of hearing stories and actually visiting these centers, there is no official documentation to produce on this, and allegations are almost impossible to prove. It is a well-kept secret. Think about it, though. If there are 4,500 beds available for placements and there are 5,100 children in need of placement, where do you put the 600 children there are no beds available for? Some of this problem is "relieved" by liberal family-court judges releasing children back into the homes they were pulled from before there is any type of case compliance by the natural parents, but that is another discussion.

The group homes found in many counties in the United States are similar but on a smaller scale. Such homes can be very therapeutic for children placed there, as they will be with other children who are going through the same sort of trauma. Such placements can be very helpful for group therapy, and allow workers and therapists to visit one location and take care of multiple cases at one time. More time can be spent on each case, as there will not be the scheduling problems and travel time that come with visiting multiple clients.

There is also a financial advantage to a group-home setting. The care expenses can be spread out among multiple placements, as the cost of running the home (other than staff) would not be much more than a single-family home. Depending on the size of the home, eight to ten placements could live there quite comfortably. This also presents advantages for high-maintenance placements, as the correct staff would be on hand to deal with the specific issues. There would also not be the problem of a mismatch between the placement and the foster family, leading to better stability for the foster child.

The downside to this type of home is the lack of a "normal" family. Additionally, there would be no family dynamic, as the only family in the home would be the other placements and paid professional workers who live in the house with them. This would not introduce a home environment, the lack of which created many of the behavior issues that the placements have. All the physical needs would be efficiently met, but I suspect that the one thing these placements need the most is the one thing that would be lacking. Unfortunately, some of the group homes here in Clark County, are not set up to provide a family dynamic; therefore, they are not considered ideal therapeutically for a foster child.

Children are placed in foster homes due to abuse and/or neglect in their biological homes. These homes are in place to provide shelter and a safe haven for foster children until they are able to return home to their biological parents or be adopted. Foster homes are ultimately a much better situation for children than a group setting, as they can receive the individual attention they need to cope with the sudden disruption in their lives that comes from being removed from their home. In a group home or foster-care center, they are more likely to be treated like just another number going through the system. Because individual homes require a larger bureaucracy for overseeing and licensing, they may not be better for states and counties, but they are definitely better for children.

Chapter 2

What to Expect as a Foster Parent

Becoming a licensed foster parent requires an extensive background check, classes, fingerprinting, a home study including a home inspection, and in many cases child CPR certification. All state child-welfare departments provide these classes for licensing, and the requirements vary from state to state. The basic requirements are a clean criminal history, enough room in the home to safely house the placement, and the ability to care for the basic needs of a child. Financial stability is also considered. Training classes are required, and this is the biggest variable from state to state. A monthly stipend is paid to the foster parent at an amount that depends on the agency and the needs and age of the child. The stipend is intended to cover the expenses of caring for the child and providing for his or her needs.

Most of the agencies throughout the United States offer special classes that focus on children with special needs. The children who are classified as "special needs" have experienced or have one or more of the following:

- sexual abuse
- post-traumatic stress disorder (PTSD)
- attention deficit/hyperactivity disorder (ADHD)
- oppositional defiant disorder (ODD)
- reactive attachment disorder (RAD)
- other psychological and/or physical handicaps

Once foster parents complete appropriate special-needs training, their home becomes a licensed therapeutic foster home. These foster parents receive a supplemented monthly stipend, depending on the age of the child, the degree of special-needs attention needed, and the private foster-care agency they become licensed through.

In Clark County, foster parents who are licensed through the county are paid the lowest monthly stipend compared to many of the local private foster-care agencies—usually about half of what other local agencies pay per child. The county that licenses homes also sets the rates that are paid to foster parents for care. If a child is considered "medically fragile" or special needs, the county will provide an extra monthly payment based on the level of the child's special needs. You will, of course, have to attend additional training classes to be awarded this extra monthly income. If you are doing foster care through a private agency, you will be paid more, because your training is much more intense and the level of care and behavior issues you will deal with are much greater.

A private agency receives its funding from the county for each child placed with it. They usually are handling cases that are too intense for a "normal" foster home to handle. This is in part because county-licensed foster homes are generally assumed to be low-maintenance, and only children with mild behavior problems should be placed in these homes. Unfortunately, many of the children who are placed in low-maintenance foster homes should actually be in a therapeutic foster home. This happens more often than not because of a shortage of foster homes, and it has become a major problem throughout the United States.

This is a recurring issue with every foster placement we have had. All foster placements come with issues and baggage, and no placement has ever been "normal," however that is defined. I would say that 50 percent of the placements we have fostered exhibited behaviors that were well above the threshold of what would be expected of a traumatized child. When we discuss placements with other foster parents, they say similar things.

Private foster-care agencies in Clark County, educate future foster parents on how to care for children with physical and mental special needs. The compensation received by foster parents is designed for use as a supplemental income to meet the daily basic needs of the child, as well as pay for transportation to and from doctor appointments, mental-health-care appointments (with psychiatrists and psychologists), additional medical and dental appointments, and weekly visitations with biological family members.

Although it's on the list of special needs, in reality, *all* children in foster care have PTSD. It would not be normal for a child under these circumstances to *not* suffer some form of trauma. This is evident because of the traumatic experience of being removed from the only family the child has ever known to be placed in a home surrounded by strangers. This has been proven with every placement in our experience with fostering. These behaviors and disorders are either mentioned on the initial intake paperwork or manifest after a week or so in the home.

When help is sought out for this, the counselors and doctors determine that there are multiple disorders present. All children we have fostered have been diagnosed with PTSD by their mental-health-care provider. Additionally, you may never know the extent of abuse or neglect that a child suffered in the original home prior to being removed. These children are confused, scared, and unable to understand why they had to leave their homes. Eventually, they begin to retaliate by acting out in ways they may not have before.

Some children withdraw from everyone, and others blame themselves for being taken from their biological home. Many of these behaviors come as a complete surprise to foster parents. They are unprepared to cope with such behaviors from their foster children, let alone any child in their care. Parents must differentiate between their biological children's "normal" behavior and a foster child's sometimes extremely aggressive behavior. Foster parents most often are left trying to figure out why a child behaves in a particular way, especially when their own children never acted out in such a way. Extreme trauma is very unpredictable and will manifest in ways that are totally unexpected.

I remember one incident just a week after our adoption of the three children we had been foster-parenting had been finalized. Our newly adopted six-year-old daughter decided she was going to settle the score with us for disciplining her the day before. She deliberately defecated on herself during the night. Early the next morning, before anyone else in the house had awakened, she proceeded to scoop her feces out of her undergarment with her hands and smear it under her brand-new bunk bed. Her reasoning as to why she didn't just go to the bathroom instead of wiping the evidence all over the bed was that she "was trying to hide it." This is just one alarming example of how the mind of a child who has suffered so many traumatic episodes in her life works.

When you become a foster parent, you are opening your home to the public eye, including teachers, principals, school staff, day-care centers, neighbors, bus drivers, doctors, nurses, and just ordinary concerned citizens. You may receive a call or a visit from CPS from time to time because one of these concerned individuals assumes that when, for example, they see your foster child eating out of the garbage, it is because you are not feeding him. There are things you can do, such as document, take photographs, and videotape—using your cell phone or video recorder—incidents that have occurred in your home. We have a video of our daughter eating one of her favorite foods and, right after she finished, going through the garbage eating who knows what. *She* didn't even know what she had put in her mouth.

People make an immediate assumption without even asking why the children eat what they do or why they cannot eat certain types of food or in many instances cannot eat at all while out in a restaurant. As a foster parent, this is something that should never come as a surprise. People are going to think what they want, and foster parents have to deal with questions, allegations, and possibly a visit from CPS.

Although you may feel as if you live in a fish bowl, you should know that the intended purpose of this is the protection of the children in foster care. As far as consistency in investigating and responding to allegations, I feel that the Department of Family Services in Clark County, is seriously slacking and chooses to randomly pick and choose certain individuals to monitor at all times. It's like wasting time watching a child suspected of shoplifting when there is an active bank robbery going on right next door. Still, you should expect to be under close examination; you will need a great deal of patience and understanding to be able to withstand the pressure that you will undoubtedly be put under.

Proper training of foster parents in what types of behavior to expect—and, more importantly, how to deal with those behaviors— would go a long way toward eliminating the abuse and other horrible things that happen to children in foster care. So would screening out those prospective foster parents who only sign up for the money and don't really care about the children. To some foster parents, taking in kids will always be a way to pay the bills.

The requirements to become a foster parent vary from state to state; however, most of the conditions are the same. Potential foster parents must be able to show that they are financially able to care for a child, despite the guarantee that they will receive a monthly allowance. They must also pass a background check—although, unfortunately, a clean background check in and of itself does not a trustworthy foster parent make. In almost all cases of child abuse, neglect, and fatalities in foster care, the foster parents had a spotless background check. In order to be licensed, every foster home must have a complete background check on every person in the home over the age of eighteen. This check includes references (seven in Nevada) as well as complete FBI, NCIS, and local law-enforcement checks. Any history of violent crime, domestic abuse, child abuse, or negative response from other sources including references will disqualify the home. Foster homes have a very high standard of background check that must be passed to be licensed. The only loophole is if something or someone has gone unreported in the official system. This can happen, but it is usually caught in one of the many interviews by various workers of either the prospective foster parents or the references listed.

This is one of the reasons the foster-care laws must be amended. Although there's no way to completely guarantee that things won't go wrong, the requirements for becoming a foster parent must become more stringent. All potential foster parents should be required to have a psychological evaluation as well as a set number of hours of anger-management classes. This may seem extreme, but if you think about it, these children are not ordinary children with typical behaviors. Foster parenting requires more than ordinary parenting skills. Remember the case of Shameeka Davis? During her trial, her lawyer had pointed out that she had multiple mental disorders, as well as suffered abuse and neglect during her own childhood. She should have never been allowed to foster children, relative or otherwise.

Three years ago, my husband and I probably would not have chosen to become foster parents if we'd had to take anger-management classes and undergo a psychiatric evaluation. If I'd known then what I know now, however, I certainly would have understood why it was necessary. I have seen children as young as three years old being rejected from a placement because they were not potty trained. Some foster parents will be placed with a child one day and tender their required ten-day notice the very next day because of behavior from the child that they do not want to deal with. Of course, I would rather see that than a child beaten to death because a foster parent was stuck with a child he or she was not mentally equipped to handle.

I remember a post on adoptionblogs.com in 2008 in which a foster parent addressed her concerns regarding changes in licensing rules, which she felt could conceivably drive foster parents away. Her first complaint was about the requirement that foster parents be fingerprinted prior to every license renewal. This complaint, I felt, was valid—your fingerprints do not change, so why require them annually or biannually? Repeat fingerprinting doesn't make sense. An arrest can change the status of a background check, so why not just conduct a background check prior to each renewal?

However, this parent also complained that social workers would now require that both parents (if applicable) be present for a scheduled visit. I do not find this unreasonable. Even a "Super Dad," as she referred to her husband, should be able to take one day off, or even half a day, for a scheduled visit once every three months. Her final grievance was about the addition of one unscheduled visit per quarter and how it could put a damper on her private life and cause a juggling of schedules. I do agree; however, when you consider the children murdered in foster care who could have been saved had this rule of "unscheduled visits" been in place years ago, scheduling concerns seem petty.

I have been physically and mentally assaulted by foster children as young as seven years old. How many people would stand idly by and allow that to happen? This in no way, shape, or form condones beating a child to death. But not everyone will be able to handle this type of situation rationally. Consequently, parents may snap and react without thinking. Many foster children are dead today for that very reason.

Shameeka Davis has stated that her foster daughter (niece), Jazzmin, was the devil, and that she feared for her seven-year-old biological daughter's safety. Shortly after Shameeka's daughter's birth, Jazzmin became jealous and began destroying the baby's clothing and other belongings. Ultimately, this resulted in Jazzmin suffering years of severe abuse that led to her untimely death. Shameeka obviously had no training in the types of behavior Jazzmin was exhibiting and did not know what to expect—or she just did not have the patience she thought she had. In many states, there are more foster children than there are foster and group homes to house them. Regardless of the children's emotional and mental status, they are placed in any foster home that is available. Regrettably, if the foster family is not physically and mentally able to address the child's needs, this could have disastrous results.

Children who are placed in foster homes come with little to no background history. This is the norm given the circumstances. However, the longer the child is in protective custody or has become a ward of the state for whatever reason, the more history the system should have on the child. Whether the parents are incarcerated, receiving inpatient or outpatient treatment for substance abuse, or whatever the case may be, foster parents should be updated (when information is available) on the status and background of the children in their home. In some cases, the placement is very temporary, lasting only a couple of days to a few weeks. Nonetheless, whatever history is available on the child should be surrendered to the foster parents so they can have some familiarity with the child's background and better understand the child's behaviors.

In Clark County, as in most states, if you foster a child or a sibling group that becomes available for adoption, you as the foster parent have the first choice of adopting that child before the state considers other adoption resources. Children who are not adopted by foster parents are first introduced on "Wednesday's Child" in order to appeal to the community for prospective adoptive families. Once you have been selected as a potential adoptive parent, you will be given a social summary packet about each child to review. "Social summary" is what it is called in Clark County; the specific name may vary from state to state. This summary packet is supposed to contain a complete medical and social history of the child during his or her time in foster care and prior to being placed in protective custody (whatever information is known and the natural parents disclose), which is usually very little. The summary is supposed to include information about services that are currently in place, such as medical, psychological, and current case plans in addition to the child's family and social history.

The summaries we received were approximately two inches thick for each child and contained reports from all the doctors and workers the children had previously seen or were currently being seen by. These were the full reports that were supposed to tell us the progress the children were making during their sessions. They also were supposed to give as complete a medical history as was known and notes from all the doctor visits they had while in foster care. The summary did contain all of this information, but a lot of it was subsequently found to be either fabricated or incomplete.

When children are in foster care, all of their medical needs are covered by Medicaid. Unfortunately, there are many doctors who only deal with foster children, as it is guaranteed money and there is an unending supply of new clients. While it is not a fair blanket accusation to make, the majority of these doctors and practitioners only supply the barest minimum care required to receive payment. We have found a few who actually are there for the best interest of the children, but they are in the minority.

The sad result is that the children do not receive the best care, and many medical issues go untreated or undiagnosed. In fairness, it must also be noted that Medicaid does not always approve treatment that is needed, which is another area of the foster system that needs to be reformed. What this does for the social summary is paint an incomplete picture of the issues the children have been treated for or are currently receiving treatment for.

A question that I am sure many would ask and we have been asked is, why would you get into something like this? The best answer is one of the reasons this book is being written: we went into it as an adoptive resource looking to adopt out of the system. We were relatively new to the foster system, and we took at face value everything that was said at all the training classes and what we had read in the literature, as well in the social summaries on the girls. We also were in it for pure and true motives of raising the children in a loving home. We were not aware of the problems that are present in the system to the degree that we know today. When we decided to do this, we thought that these were for the most part normal children who needed a good, safe, and secure place to receive love and stability.

We were aware that there would be some challenges and some issues with the neglect, abuse, and abandonment experienced by the children in the system. However, the degree to which this affected the children was not fully explained to or expected by us. This lack of information contributes to the number of failed adoptions and "returned" placements in the foster system. It also helps explain why there is abuse, neglect, and murder within the system by the caretakers. If there was full disclosure (or as much as is known) of every issue and problem associated with a child, and children were classified according to their true needs, these issues would be drastically reduced.

Our home is licensed as a regular foster home. Until the children we adopted were placed with us for the required six months prior to adoption, they were in therapeutic foster care for children with special needs and behavioral problems. Since we hadn't taken the classes and gotten licensed as a therapeutic home ourselves, I don't think we should have been considered for adoption of these children. The county is so desperate to place children in adoptive homes that they will place children with any parents who show an interest regardless of whether they have been trained on what to expect or how to deal with these types of children.

Why did we stick with it and not call it off and become another statistic of a failed adoption? It is very hard to give up once a child is placed in your home. These children did not exhibit erratic behavior beyond what we would expect from any child who has been through what they have. The child-welfare system did not fully disclose to us all the issues that were known and the severity of them. We found out after the adoption was final and then started asking more questions of the former foster mother. That is when a lot of what we know today started to come to light, and we have been finding out more every day.

Volumes could be written about what we have gone through and continue to battle every day. Our case and issues are not unique, as I have spoken with many foster parents and compared notes. While the children we foster are seeing their parents during visits, I am usually talking to other foster parents about their issues and problems with not only the children they take care of but also the caseworkers, courts, and birth parents. I have yet to find a foster parent who does not agree with anything that will be or has been discussed in this book. It is our motivation, and I find it is the motivation of other foster parents, that they do it for the good of the children and to provide a service that is so desperately needed in the community. This in spite of a system that is stacked against foster parents, even though the system needs us more than anyone admits.

In no way do I want to discourage anyone from becoming a foster parent. It can be one of the most rewarding and selfless things you will ever do in your life. Before you make any decisions, though, much consideration has to be given to exactly why you want to do this and the resources it will consume in time, money, freedom, and frustration. Beginning the process of becoming a foster parent can be exhausting, to say the least. If you don't like the rules that are in place, this may not be the right avenue for you.

To be successful as a foster parent, you must be very patient and understanding, love children, and not be in it for the money. This is not something that can be taken on as a hobby or something that "might be fun to do." It is a lot of work and requires great demands on your time. If you do not go into this with full disclosure and due diligence, you will find that you have set yourself up for a great deal of disappointment and frustration. If you lack the required patience and understanding, you or your foster child could become a statistic.

Chapter 3

Fostering to Adopt

When you are making a decision to adopt a child or children who have been fostered, the social summary is often the only information available regarding the history of the children other than personal observations made while fostering prior to adoption. Unfortunately, extreme behaviors may not become readily apparent until after the adoption has been finalized.

This is another area of the foster-care system that needs reform and more truth in reporting. Anyone who adopts from the foster-care system should be aware that there are going to be issues with the children who are available for adoption. The purpose of the social summary is to inform prospective adoptive parents of the type and severity of these issues. If the summaries were truthful and outlined the complete history of these children, there would be less chance of a bad match in the adoption.

If after reviewing the social summary the foster parents make the decision to move forward with the process of adopting the child, the next step is to attend a CFT (Child and Family Team) meeting prior to the child or children being placed in their home. The participants in this meeting may include any or all of the following individuals: the child's caseworker, a court-appointed social advocate for the child (CASA), the child's psychosocial rehabilitator (PSR), the child's psychologist, biological family members unable to adopt the child, and any other persons who have an interest in the child's welfare. The purpose of the CFT meeting is for all parties involved to get acquainted, discuss the status of the child (including any concerns or problems that the potential adoptive parents will need to know about), go over any services that are currently in place, and discuss long-term care plans.

The decision to adopt a child after you have fostered him or her for six months is based solely on the contents of the social summary and the child's behavior while in your home. You can, of course, decide to not go through with the adoption after the six-month waiting period (failed adoption). In my opinion, you can bond with a child within six months, but it usually takes that long or longer just to get to know him or her. A year with a child prior to adoption is not unreasonable; you will then have gotten to know his or her behaviors and how to deal with them.

The Department of Family Services pushed us to finalize the adoption of our children right at the six-month mark despite our request to postpone for a few more months. If their intention is to ensure that these children are successfully placed, this is not the way to do it. This may very well be why there are so many failed adoptions. The first six months is like the honeymoon period. You cannot get to know a child or expect a child to get to know you sufficiently in a six-month period to make a lifetime commitment. Think about it. Do you think children are going to show their true behavior or have an opportunity to react to every trigger that will set off unexplained behavior in six months? Probably not.

The social summaries we received on our children were, at the very least, outdated, and later they were found to be not 100 percent accurate. This, I am sure, was not an isolated incident. Our decision to adopt was based on false information in our children's social summaries. We were not fostering them at the time we received their summaries, so we were not able to experience their behaviors firsthand. Furthermore, the foster home before ours was a therapeutic foster home, the type of home into which our children really should have been placed for adoption.

This is a very big problem in the state of Nevada, and it explains a lot about why a large number of adoptions through the foster-care system fail. We watch the available children for adoption on a regular basis as well as talk to many of the caseworkers we know and ask about the children we see. It is unfortunate that we see so many of the same children be put on the pending adoption list only to reappear as available six months later. When the real story comes to light, it always seems the adoptive family was not aware of the behavioral issues that were present and the family just couldn't deal with it. There should be a law in place mandating that children with special needs can only be placed in therapeutic foster homes. This would also ensure that children available for adoption are placed in adoptive homes prepared to deal with what could best be described as irrational behavior.

If there are not enough of these types of homes to accommodate children with special needs, then all foster homes should be licensed for both special-needs and non-special-needs. Foster parents would then be compensated monthly based on the type of children they fostered the month prior. With this rule in place, all children could be placed in any foster home available. Although any foster parent has the option to decline a placement, at least with a law in place requiring all foster homes to be licensed for all types of foster-care needs, any available foster home would be equipped to handle any child's needs.

Parents who are considering adopting children internationally, especially children living in orphanages, should be required to follow these same state guidelines, to include CPR certification. Although you do not have the benefit of fostering the children before adopting, at least you can be prepared in the event of an unforeseen circumstance. Additionally, parents should be required to take at least a minimum forty-hour class on caring for children with special needs. When adopting internationally, such as from Russia, you may have little to no history on the children or their parentage. Tragically, between 1996 and 2010, fifteen Russian children who were adopted by American families were killed by their adoptive parents. This could possibly have been prevented if certain laws had been in place. Unfortunately, it is no different for the children here in the US foster-care system.

The next few pages detail the most recent trends in foster care and adoption, between FY 2002 and FY 2010. The information is provided by AFCARS, and includes a chart showing the time between termination of parental rights (TPR) to finalization of adoption, determined by each state's guidelines, during FY October 1, 2009, to September 30, 2010. The good news is that there has been a decline in the number of children in foster care between FY 2002 and FY 2010. While these are national figures, they will apply in proportion to most areas of the United States. Unfortunately, the number of children waiting to be adopted, or for whom parental rights have been terminated, has increased. The number of children who were actually adopted has fluctuated during those eight years, yet those numbers were not extreme. This is the most recent data compiled at the time of this writing for the United States.

Trends in Foster Care and Adoption—FY 2002–FY 2010
(Based on data submitted by states as of June 2011)

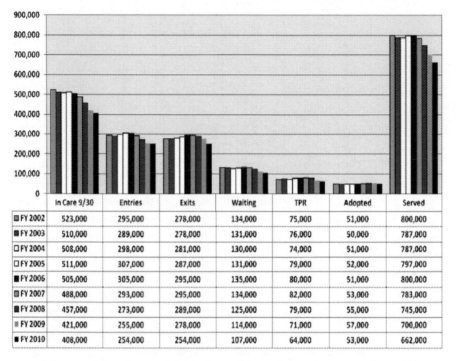

	In Care 9/30	Entries	Exits	Waiting	TPR	Adopted	Served
FY 2002	523,000	295,000	278,000	134,000	75,000	51,000	800,000
FY 2003	510,000	289,000	278,000	131,000	76,000	50,000	787,000
FY 2004	508,000	298,000	281,000	130,000	74,000	51,000	787,000
FY 2005	511,000	307,000	287,000	131,000	79,000	52,000	797,000
FY 2006	505,000	305,000	295,000	135,000	80,000	51,000	800,000
FY 2007	488,000	293,000	295,000	134,000	82,000	53,000	783,000
FY 2008	457,000	273,000	289,000	125,000	79,000	55,000	745,000
FY 2009	421,000	255,000	278,000	114,000	71,000	57,000	700,000
FY 2010	408,000	254,000	254,000	107,000	64,000	53,000	662,000

FFY = Federal Fiscal Year (October 1 through September 30)

Subpopulation Definitions

1. **In Care 9/30**: This is an estimated count of all the children in foster care *on the last day* of the FFY. An individual child is included in the count for each year for which he or she is in foster care on the last day.
2. **Entries**: This is an estimated count of all children who entered foster care *during* the FFY. An individual child is counted only once for each year, even if the child entered, exited, and reentered care during the year. The most recent date of removal from home is used to determine whether the child entered foster care during the period. If an individual child entered in one

year and then exits and reenters in a subsequent year, he or she is included in the count of entries for both years.

3. **Exits**: This is an estimated count of all children who exited foster care during the FFY *at the end of their most recent foster-care episode*. An individual child is counted only once for each year, even if the child exited, reentered, and exited again during the year. The most recent date of discharge (from foster care) is the one counted. If an individual child exited care in one year and then reenters and exits again in a subsequent year, he or she is included in the count of exits for both years.

4. **Waiting**: This is an estimated count of all children who are waiting to be adopted *on the last day* of the FFY. An individual child is included in the count for each year in which he or she is waiting to be adopted on the last day. There is no federal definition for children waiting to be adopted. For the purposes of this analysis, children waiting to be adopted include children with a goal of adoption and/or whose parental rights have been terminated. The "waiting" population excludes children whose parents' rights have been terminated, who are sixteen years old and older, and who have a goal of emancipation. An individual child is included in the count for each year that he or she has these characteristics on the last day of the year.

5. **TPR (Termination of Parental Rights)**: This is an estimated count of all children in care *on the last day* of the FFY whose parental rights have been terminated and who are waiting for adoption. An individual child who has these characteristics on the last day of the year is counted only once for that year.

6. **Adopted**: This is an estimated count of all children adopted with public child welfare agency involvement *during the FFY*. An individual child is counted only once for each year, even if (in rare cases) the child was adopted multiple times during the year. In cases when an individual child is adopted in one year and then adopted again in a subsequent year, he or she is included in the count of adoptions for both years.

7. **Served**: This is an estimated count of all children who were in the public foster-care system *during the FFY*. This number is the sum of two mutually exclusive groups of children: the children

who are already in care on the first day of the fiscal year (as of October 1) and the children who enter foster care during the year. An individual child is counted only once for each year.

Source: AFCARS data, US Children's Bureau, Administration for Children, Youth, and Families, http://www.acf.hhs.gov/sites/default/files/cb/trends_fostercare_adoption.pdf.

Chapter 4

What Happens When You Are Accused of Abuse

In foster-training classes, you are told that as foster parents, you will always be under a great deal of scrutiny. Foster parents are automatically stereotyped as greedy swindlers, providing their services for the financial gain that comes along with it and nothing else. This is not the case with many foster families, including ours. However, you have to be prepared to deal with individuals who are not convinced that there are foster parents out there who only have good intentions.

According to our children's former caseworker, all children in foster care are manipulative in such a way that they will do whatever it takes to get what they want. If a child accuses you of neglect and/or abuse, it will be investigated. Foster parents are not allowed to spank foster children, nor can any other corporal punishment be used on them. Children who have been in the foster system for a while know this rule all too well, because the system trains them on how to manipulate. When one of our children told me she hated me, I told her that I did not feel the same way toward her. She then piped up with, "Well, you are just saying that because you are supposed to!"

My greatest fear as a child was of being spanked. I feared my mother more than my father, because my father did not spank us—so of course, he was the one I really took advantage of, in more ways than one. This is exactly what foster children do when they know they cannot be spanked. While we were still fostering our children, our daughter would tell us all the time that we were not allowed to spank her, and if we did, she was going to tell on us. When children know they cannot be spanked, they will act out in the most unimaginable ways. After all, what's the worst thing that can happen? They get placed in time-out for a few minutes to think about what they have done? This is another reason children are shuffled from one foster home to the next. I am not condoning corporal punishment by any means; there are more stringent age-appropriate consequences that do not involve corporal punishment that are as effective when a child misbehaves.

One of our adopted children—who, according to her former caseworker, has reactive attachment disorder (RAD) along with other psychological disorders—is very manipulative. This same former caseworker saw our family at a dental appointment while there with her own children, and she decided to get our daughter alone to ask about a mark on her face. She then decided to utilize her county employment status by flashing her social-worker badge to the front-desk staff in order to get our daughter in the back office to do her questioning. She also instructed the staff to keep us in the waiting area.

This caseworker did act in good faith by using the Social Workers Code of Ethics initially. However, when this woman was able to speak to our daughter alone to question her about the mark, the caseworker proceeded to ask her if she wanted her back in her life. That was when this woman broke the code of ethics! Why would you ask a child if she wants someone back in her life when—as you have been the one to point out—the child is very manipulative and has RAD? Our daughter, of course, *did* want this caseworker back in her life, so she said what she felt she had to do to make that happen. She explained the mark on her face by telling her former caseworker that I had pushed her.

Needless to say, CPS came out to our home the very next day to investigate our daughter's claims. After talking with all the family members living in the home, they found no evidence that our daughter had been abused or neglected, something we already knew. In fact, our daughter had made the same claim on several occasions. She has admitted that she lies about abuse to get people to feel sorry for her. Although we have adopted her, we remain under the same scrutiny as when we fostered her and her siblings.

I am an avid believer in following up on children's claims of abuse, because it is impossible at first to know when or if they are crying wolf. However, there are always two sides to a story, and that was no different in the case of our daughter. She was convinced that if she made up a story, she would be able to go back to being a foster child, where she could manipulate the system and receive the attention she loved so much. Our daughter gets attached to people very easily because of her

RAD, and she knows how to manipulate people to get what she wants. Many children in foster care are manipulative, because in many ways this is their means of survival.

Incidentally, our daughter has a psychological disorder that leads her to perform self-mutilation of different parts of her body, and for sympathy she will lie to anyone who empathizes with her plight. The result of this is that Mom, Dad, or some other unsuspecting adult who may have crossed her is accused of abusing her. One solution that we had found to help us document her issues is to take photographs of her body every night before she goes to bed; in the morning, we take photographs and videotape any part of her body where there is a new bruise or mark. Unfortunately, we have realized that this is too much trouble, and we feel that the cameras we have installed throughout the home are sufficient. The cameras have worked wonders, as most of the behaviors are happening during the daytime. Furthermore, she has since curbed her self-mutilation behaviors significantly.

Many who visit our home have commented on the security system we have installed and ask the purpose of this level of security. Other than the obvious reasons of burglary protection, video provides indisputable evidence of anything that happens in the house. Cameras are aimed at all entrances and common areas, such as the family room and kitchen. Not only do these cameras provide evidence of outside threats coming in, they also provide evidence of what happens with the children and any issues that might come up regarding them. Many think it is for the protection of the children in the house from wrongful behavior of babysitters and/or nannies. Most are surprised when we explain they are not for the children's protection, but for our protection from false accusations and to show workers the behaviors we talk about.

You may ask how it affects the day-to-day routine in the house to have a camera watch and record every move. It has no effect on anything, as the cameras are completely forgotten about until we need to review footage to see what happened after an incident. After all, when we're out in public at any store or on most roads, every move is being watched. Surveillance cameras have become so commonplace that nobody notices them.

The photos and videos have helped us curb our daughter's manipulation considerably. We also have medical documentation by a licensed psychiatrist to go with our own documentation in the form of pictures, videotapes, and recorded interviews. This is very important if you ever have to prove your innocence in an abuse case against you— you absolutely must have documentation from a psychiatrist in order to build a strong case, if it should get to that point. Unfortunately, there are not many people who would feel it's worth the trouble.

We know that without our determination to give her a chance, our daughter might have ended up either in an abusive home or as one of those statistics of foster children who were killed because their foster parents did not have the patience to understand their needs. Most likely, she would have bounced from home to home in foster care or from failed adoption to failed adoption, until she aged out in the system. At that time, she would have been put out into the world with no sense of belonging, carrying all her baggage and psychological damage from never having a stable home to belong to. It is very sad that many foster children suffer this plight.

Incidentally, after our visit from CPS, we were told that we would receive a Report of Disposition letter stating that the case was closed, because of claims being unsubstantiated within two weeks from the date of their visit. We did receive the letter . . . ten months later. It was dated ten months prior. Since then, we have had two wards in our home for almost that same amount of time. This is a classic example of how the system is broken and cannot track its own cases.

The Division of Child and Family Services in Nevada, and every other state for that matter, is not the only entity that places foster parents under a microscope. Many of the services that are in place for foster children, especially those that are very familiar with the monthly payments that foster parents receive to care for the children, are very observant of children's behaviors in the home and how foster or adoptive parents handle these behaviors. We, as well as many other foster parents we have had the opportunity to talk to, have contemplated many times whether or not we should renew our license each year because of lack of support from Family Services. As a foster parent, you are forced to resort to any number and manner of complaints from biological family members regarding the children you are fostering during their scheduled visits. Then there are the complaints by other sources that claim to be looking out for the best interest of the child, such as CASA (court appointed special advocate), PSR (psycho-social rehabilitation), BST (basic skills trainer), and the general public, as well as other inconveniences that continue to plague your life.

This is the reality of foster care under the current system. It is not meant to discourage anyone from fostering, as there are many rewards, but an informed decision with all facts present must be made prior to committing to caring for the needs of what for the most part are innocent children who have been damaged by circumstances out of their control. At the end of the day, our children will still be with us healthy, alive, and well for years to come.

All foster children we have taken care of have come to us with eating problems, such as hoarding their food and in some cases gorging until they threw it up. Hiding food, eating food out of the garbage, and eating stale, inedible food are also classic symptoms that show up. These are among the many survival tactics that foster children utilize. They may have come from a home where they were not fed on a regular basis or didn't know when or if they were going to receive their next meal. Many foster parents do not know this, which can create serious problems with a placement. Most onlookers automatically assume that when they see a child eating out of the garbage or stealing food, that child is not being fed in his or her current home. That is an understandable assumption, especially when these well-meaning people ask the child why he or she is doing this and the child replies simply, "I'm hungry." As a foster parent, you will be judged by your alleged lack of concern for the child, and you may just receive a visit from CPS. Having a foster child with eating issues creates a very difficult situation for foster parents.

All the children we have fostered for more than a month, including the children we adopted, have had eating problems. They have stolen food, eaten out of the trash, and/or eaten spoiled food. The children we adopted were eating three breakfasts at three different locations a day for over four months until we finally realized what was going on. They would eat breakfast at home; they would go to a before-and-after-school day-care program and eat breakfast there; and then they would eat breakfast at school. They were able to get away with this because foster children receive free meals at school, and even after adoption, our children still receive limited public assistance, which included continued free school meals. When asked why they did it, they would simply reply, "I was hungry."

They were finally caught when our oldest ended up in the school nurse's office throwing up violently. You could actually see what she'd eaten, including what her teacher had just scolded her for eating—an expired cinnamon roll that somebody had given her. We were able to put two and two together and figure out what was going on, but by then it was too late. Shortly thereafter, we removed our children from school permanently. All three girls have a genetic intestinal condition. Since the incident with the school nurse, two of them have had colonoscopies, at eight and nine years of age. Our oldest has, to date, had two colonoscopies and endoscopies combined. She also was diagnosed with Crohn's disease. Our second oldest has an abnormality in her colon that was detected during the colonoscopy, and she was recently diagnosed with thyroid disease to add to her other medical conditions. Our youngest has exhibited symptoms of diabetes, and like our middle child is currently under the care of a pediatric endocrinologist. All three children are also under the care of a pediatric gastroenterologist and are on a very strict diet.

The problem occurs when people do not look at the whole picture, only part of it. Children who enter into foster care already come with excess baggage, including these eating problems. This may be where the "neglect" part of the abuse comes in, as many of them are abandoned and left for days to fend for themselves, or even may have been homeless with their family prior to being removed from their home. This is how they learn to survive, by rummaging through the garbage for food.

The bizarre twist in all of this is the number of children who have died at the hands of their foster/adopted parents who at the time of their death were found to be malnourished. Some of these children are taken from their biological home where they were deprived of food and placed in a foster home where they were being denied food! Where is the logic in that?

Chapter 5

Death from CPS Neglect

Most of us think of CPS as a safe haven for abused and neglected children. This agency and its workers are supposed to protect children from harm. We consider the caseworkers to be trustworthy and wouldn't think twice about calling them when we suspect abuse. Yet according to an article in the Ft. Lauderdale, Florida, *Sun Sentinel* written by Yvonne Mason, CPS investigators have failed children in more than one instance.

One case that drew media attention in Florida in 2011 was that of Nubia and Victor Barahona. This sad story is about how one beautiful little girl and her brother were abused by their foster parents and Florida CPS, which ultimately resulted in her death. All of the signs of abuse at the hands of Nubia and Victor's foster parents were reported appropriately. Not once were the allegations of abuse ever followed up on by CPS. Florida's state law designates teachers and guidance counselors as being mandatory reporters of abuse and neglect of a child. They can face prosecution if they do not report their suspicions to CPS. When several school staff members *did* follow protocol by reporting what they saw as signs of abuse, they were all but ignored. When CPS followed up, they reported justifiable reasons for the signs reported by school staff. Because of this, the staff's reports were not taken seriously. Here we have another tragic end to a child's life. Had there been one response to the complaints on the many calls that flooded in to CPS, and had they been acted upon, Nubia might be alive today.

Foster and adoptive parents are supposed to pass a rigorous background check, but this was not the case for Renée Bowman. Two years after a misdemeanor conviction in 1999 for threatening a seventy-two-year-old man, she filed for bankruptcy protection—and was still able to foster children the very same year that she filed! Look at that again. Convicted for threatening a seventy-two-year-old man and still able to foster, and then adopt a sibling group of three children two years later. This is a conviction for a violent act, and at the least shows the propensity for this type of behavior. (While the conviction was only for a threat, the real crime was not revealed and may have been pled down from something more serious.) It also shows a tendency to prey on the weak and helpless. Adopting a child who may have behavior issues is not in the best interest of someone with this mind-set, nor is it the safest and most stable environment for the child. Bowman later was convicted of murdering two of her three adopted daughters and hiding their bodies in a freezer for more than six months while still receiving monthly payments for them.

Foster parents are supposed to receive frequent visits by caseworkers to ensure the safety and well-being of the children, but that did not protect the niece and nephew of Shameeka Davis. The family lived in Antioch, California, but Davis's foster-care home was under the supervision of the San Francisco Human Services Agency. Because she had been providing a home for her nephew and niece, who were twins, since they were toddlers, San Francisco officials felt that the home must be stable enough, and a caseworker was only required to visit the home once every six months. These visits were scheduled, with some arranged two to three weeks in advance and frequently canceled and rescheduled by Davis herself. The surviving sibling (the nephew) has said that he knew when it was getting close to the biannual visits because his aunt would feed them again and treat their scars and injuries (from the abuse) with medicines and bleaching creams. I am convinced that this would not have happened—and Davis would not have had the opportunity to murder her niece, Jazzmin—had San Francisco's Human Services Agency required quarterly unscheduled visits in addition to the monthly visits, and not relied on the fact that since she was a long-term relative placement, everything had to be okay. Furthermore, I find it hard to believe that the caseworker actually had physical face-to-face contact with both children, because if she had, she would have seen the abuse firsthand. In my opinion, she turned a blind eye, which cost one of the children her life.

Unfortunately, we know all too well that these are not isolated incidents. Abuse and neglect claims have gone ignored by CPS in other states as well. Oklahoma had reports prior to five child deaths that could have been prevented had CPS acted. Shockingly, in a 2009 report, 55 percent of abuse and neglect allegations in foster care did not receive further investigation because DHS (the Department of Human Services) felt that it was not warranted. Both CPS and OCA (Office of Client Advocacy) are notorious for disregarding credible evidence of abuse or neglect in the home.

On the other hand, I have seen some instances where even an ounce of suspicion of child abuse has been acted upon almost immediately. A possible issue in the inconsistency of response by CPS is that it may be dependent upon who is doing the reporting. A mandatory reporter is going to get more attention than a neighbor calling in, especially if it is not the first time a concern was called in by the same person. If the first call was cleared, it will probably be assumed it is just an upset neighbor trying to get back at the foster parents for something. A mandatory reporter should get immediate response because of the higher level of contact with the alleged victim, especially if it's a teacher or social worker. Whatever the reason, the inconsistency with CPS's protocol has created an uproar.

The actions or lack of action of CPS has resulted in a nationwide outrage. We the taxpayers feel the brunt of it every time the agency is sued. In March 2012, a $170,000 settlement was approved by the Las Vegas County Commissioner after the 2006 death of a seven-month-old baby boy at the hands of his foster mother, Melanie Ochs. Additionally, the twin brother of fifteen-year-old Jazzmin Davis, who was brutally murdered by her aunt Shameeka Davis who was also her foster mother, sued the San Francisco Department of Child Protective Services for $4 million. If we cannot rely on CPS to protect our children, who can we rely on?

We have experienced a decrease in the quality of service by some of our licensing workers and our children's caseworkers, probably in part due to high caseloads and staff shortages. This has had a grave impact on the care of foster children in foster homes. Caseworkers should listen to the foster parents as well as the children when it comes to concerns and behavior issues. The monthly visits are a requirement, but they are put in place to afford caseworkers the opportunity to observe any changes in the children's demeanor and behaviors from month to month, as well as to hear any concerns from the foster parents.

Perhaps if the caseworkers were given a lighter load and more caseworkers were hired to handle the demand, tragedy could be averted in most if not all cases. If the caseworkers were allowed to spend time not only on their *scheduled* visits but also on random unannounced visits whenever they wanted to, I am convinced that many more cases of abuse in foster homes could be detected. They already have the right to make such visits, but in practice they do not have the time to do so because of overly heavy caseloads. Jazzmin Davis might be alive today if caseworkers had dropped in when her aunt Shameeka was not expecting them.

In our experience as foster parents, we have only had one random visit, and that was on a day when we were not home. Even if we had been there, one of the girls would have been in school. This presents another issue that prevents visits like these from occurring and being effective. If school-age children are involved, the times that visits like these can happen in the home are limited. Visiting the school is always possible, but that can be very disruptive and scary for the child as well as the school.

Clark County, requires that foster parents submit a ten-day notice to DFS if they are no longer willing or able to care for their foster child. This ten-day rule should be a courtesy only. If a child is in a home where he or she is not wanted or does not want to be, there is going to be a great deal of tension in that home. Forcing children to remain in a home where they are not wanted is like imprisoning them for ten days. Is this really in the best interest of the child?

After an adoption is finalized (usually six months after the child is placed), visits from the caseworker and CASA worker abruptly stop. This is like taking drugs away from an addict cold turkey. No weaning, no nothing. Imagine the adverse effect this could have on a child with RAD, particularly since most of these children have already lost so many people in their lives who had promised to be there for them. It would be so much easier for children to acclimate to a new home and family if they knew that their caseworker would still come by periodically for visits.

Adopted children should be followed by DFS for at least two years after the adoption is finalized. In that two-year time period, there should be a minimum of four visits (two per year). These should include at least one unscheduled visit each year. Additional visits should follow every second or third year until the child turns eighteen. This law should be enforced for all adoptive parents, with some leniency. I believe it should be strictly enforced for those parents who continue to receive a monthly adoption subsidy for their children.

If this seems unreasonable to some, let us not forget Renée Bowman, the woman who killed two of her children and hid their bodies in a freezer for more than six months while still receiving monthly payments for them. I guess she figured since the girls were technically still in her home, although dead and in a frozen state, she had the right to continue receiving the subsidy checks.

When children die at the hands of their foster parents, it would be interesting to know what the reports said in their caseworker's previous month's visit. A good caseworker should be able to pick up any sign of abuse, whether verbal or physical. For children who are unable to speak for themselves because they are not old enough to talk or because of a speech impediment, caseworkers should be required to be more attentive to these children's behaviors. Incidentally, if some of these children are talking to their teachers and school officials about the goings-on in their home, why aren't the caseworkers able to get them to talk?

Part of the reason for this shortcoming on the caseworkers' part is the amount of time spent with the children during each visit and the time between visits. Human memory being what it is, and taking into account the number of clients seen by each caseworker each month, it is no wonder that caseworkers are not reporting or even seeing the real situation. It may well be that they do not have the time to spend in the home and, on top of that, are not taking good notes. Making six to ten visits in a day, going back to the office and trying to organize the events of the day, and then trying to recall what the overall condition of each child was the month before would be a daunting task for anyone.

The other problem caseworkers face is the amount of time allotted for a visit. Before children will talk, they need to feel comfortable and trust the person they are talking to. It's not possible to build that trust in a half-hour visit, and the children are not going to open up and say anything if there is an issue going on in the home. Large sibling groups in the same home complicate matters even more. I know foster parents who have housed a sibling group of six children. If a caseworker were to really do his or her job when conducting monthly visits, it would take at least half a work day to do a sibling group of that size. This does not happen.

The tragedies that have occurred over the years because of CPS's shortcomings have culminated in several lawsuits against them, and there is a considerably growing number of people and attorneys pushing for class-action suits against DPSS, DFS, and HRS as well. These lawsuits will not bring these children back. Hopefully, it may provide some peace of mind to the surviving family and friends of the victims. The extent of the lawsuits is disheartening at minimum. Unfortunately, there doesn't seem to be any improvement with the system to date. Had CPS and all of the entities that fall under its umbrella consistently followed appropriate guidelines and department procedures, they would not be under scrutiny today. These guidelines include proper and timely visits, responding to the reports of foster parents regarding behaviors of children, and providing the treatment and help the children need. CPS also needs to put more resources into the well-being and safety of the children instead of the rehabilitation of the birthparents.

Putting the needs of the birthparents before those of the children is one of the things that cause death and abuse. Once children are placed in a foster home, barring any medical issues that come up, the rest of the case is about the parents. The children are for the most part ignored, and their needs and concerns are not always provided for. This places the burden of the children's problems on the foster parents. If they are not equipped or are not given the resources to deal with this, they will become overwhelmed—and can lose their cool and take it out on the children.

Chapter 6

No Support for Foster Parents

As parents who both work full-time outside the home, we have always felt a lack of support from DFS when it came to being foster parents. This has been expressed in many ways, but here we are going to talk about the lack of financial support for caring for foster children with any type of special needs during the day when both parents are working.

In Clark County, working foster parents can apply for child care through a subsidized program. This is the same program low-income families are also eligible to apply for. Our children have always been approved at a 100 percent rate based on state guidelines, but that never covered the entire weekly day-care fee unless our children were going part-time.

This was not the worst thing we had to deal with regarding this program. The process is long and confusing, because you are not told everything you need to know about the application process and how long the wait times are until payment is disbursed to the center. At one point, we had to pay for all three of our children's summer program for two of the three months before we were reimbursed. Washoe County in Northern Nevada does not reimburse working parents for day-care services, as I am sure many other counties throughout the United States don't. Instead, they choose to place school-aged children in these homes. If both parents are working, I am sure they either leave for work before school starts or get off from work after school has let out for the day. If this is the case, who is watching the children during that time when the parents are not there?

This also brings up concerns in the placement process. If dual-working parents can only take school-aged children, they are limiting the age of the children, which could result in a large number of poorly placed children. We have lost several placements because we were not able to take a child right away but needed to first make day-care arrangements prior to accepting the placement. In the end, the children lose.

Day-care centers and providers should not charge foster parents the balance of the day-care fees that are not paid by the county, in my opinion. This would also include schools that offer before- and after-school care programs. Some people may think that the income foster parents receive to care for the child should be used to pay for day care. Unfortunately, with the cost of day care, it would use up our entire monthly supplement. If the county feels excess day-care fees should be paid for by the foster parents, those parents should receive supplemental income in addition to their regular monthly subsidized payment.

We keep close track of the money that is paid to us for foster care, even setting up a separate bank account just for those funds. I can assure you that it does not cover all the expenses associated with the care of our foster children. We also do not cut corners when it comes to clothing, food, and toys, and we do not use respite when we travel. We always take our foster placements with us wherever we go. We feel it gives them a better sense of belonging and stability rather than uprooting them to another home for a week while we go out of town.

In October 2009, the *Oregonian* reported that a compensation overhaul would result in many foster parents receiving a raise in their monthly reimbursement checks. The downside to this was that those caring for children with medical special needs experienced a cut in their payments—as much as half of what they were receiving. This action inevitably caused some foster parents to give up caring for children with special needs. Ultimately, many of them threatened to quit foster parenting altogether. At press time, I am unaware of any actions of this type being documented.

In Clark County, some foster-care agencies that offer larger monthly reimbursements for children with special needs require that at least one of the parents not work outside the home. The reason is so the children will receive the one-on-one attention and care they need. Moreover, this enables the parent to transport the child to and from medical appointments and therapy sessions. Some of these children may have multiple appointments a day. As mentioned earlier in this chapter, foster parents who run therapeutic foster homes rely solely on these checks to provide for the physical, emotional, and medical assistance these children require. If these payments are reduced, this would inevitably reduce needed medical treatments.

If other states follow Oregon's reduction in reimbursement rates to therapeutic foster families, this will eventually result in an even greater decline in available foster homes for the children who need them most. This may result in many children being institutionalized, as there will be more children with special needs requiring foster-home placement than foster homes available to accommodate them.

Chapter 7

Health-Care Services in Foster Care

Medical and dental services furnished to foster children and children adopted from foster care are provided by the state. Each child receives a Medicaid card with an assigned Medicaid number. There are providers that are contracted through the county to provide services to these children.

Our experience with Medicaid has been one of false promises. We were told that once our children were adopted, Medicaid would cover all the necessary medical expenses until they reached the age of eighteen. This turned out to be a big lie. We added them to our own health-care policy, and immediately the services we were promised were denied because Medicaid was now secondary and our primary insurance would not cover all of these services. We were told that if our insurance did not cover what was needed, Medicaid would take care of it. This is not the case. The lesson learned here is not to add adopted children to your private health insurance. At the next open enrollment opportunity, they will be dropped from our policy. I should be fair and say that with very few exceptions, the services for foster children have always been provided. The only exception to this has been some mental-health services.

Prior to our children being placed in our home, we were informed in the initial CFT meeting of medical and dental services that were currently in place. The former foster mother lived about thirty miles from us, and our girls' pediatrician, dentist, and psychologist lived in her vicinity. We felt that in order to maintain some continuity with our girls' health-care providers, they would continue to see those doctors at least until the adoption was finalized. It was a big mistake for us to even think that.

When we first met our three girls, they had very poor hygiene. Two of them were overweight, and they all had severe eating problems. This was quite surprising to us, because they had been in foster care for two years before coming into our home. You would think that their hygiene, weight, and eating issues would have been addressed by then. Our oldest daughter, who was eight years old at the time, tipped the scales at a whopping ninety-six pounds! I was even more shocked when we took our children to the pediatrician for their required "within two weeks well check" after entering a new foster home. The pediatrician never addressed concerns regarding our daughter's weight, which baffled me. I made the decision to devise a healthy eating and exercise plan that was age-appropriate for all of our children, which included eliminating carbonated sodas altogether. This was something they were used to drinking almost daily. All three of them are now at a healthy weight for their age.

This brings up the question of who is responsible for their condition. Do we put the blame on Medicaid for not following up on patient treatment or looking at medical records prior to payment, or do we place the responsibility on the doctor for not giving competent medical services? I blame them both. It is the doctor's duty to provide proper medical care to all who are seen, regardless of whether the patient has private insurance, public insurance like Medicaid, or an inability to pay. In this case, it was pretty clear that there was at the least some questionable billing on the part of the doctor and clearly no oversight on the part of Medicaid. The medical record shows that our eight-year-old daughter's weight was clearly off the growth chart, yet there was never any mention of a concern from the physician or Medicaid—if they even viewed her medical records like they should have.

Medicaid is the US health program for families and individuals with low income and resources. It is a means-tested program that is jointly funded by the state and federal government managed by the states. People served by Medicaid are US citizens or legal permanent residents, including low-income adults, their children, and people with certain disabilities. That being said, there is a fiduciary responsibility on the part of doctors to the public at large that funds this system. In a situation like the one we experienced with that doctor, the responsibility to the public was certainly not met.

This is one example of the waste and fraud in the Medicaid system. According to the records of our children's prior pediatrician, they were seen by her on a day when in fact we were out of town on vacation. Her records state that she talked with me about our girls eating healthy and making good choices on the right kinds of foods to eat. We have a three-page medical history for this one visit that is completely made up of false statements. We did take our children to see her, but not until the following week. Additionally, had she truly discussed these issues with me, the obvious morbid obesity health risk for our oldest daughter would have definitely come up. This is just one physician we have had suspicious dealings with.

Before our children could receive psychological care, they needed approval through Medicaid to determine whether psych services were medically necessary. Our oldest daughter was continually denied services because she simply "wouldn't talk." Eventually she would be approved, but not for the full services she desperately needed. Services were good for three months only, at which time the mental-health providers had to submit a new case plan for each child. Our two youngest were never denied because their actions were more extroverted and they craved negative attention.

I never will understand what qualifies any individual or an organization like Medicaid to determine a foster child's psychological needs based on the fact that he or she won't talk. Do people not realize that when someone, especially a child, withdraws from others, it could very well be because she has been traumatized or even abused? Our oldest received the least amount of psychological care for this reason, yet we found out less than two months after she was placed in our home that she had in fact been sexually molested by a former foster father. This incident had happened in their very first foster-home placement.

Approximately five months after she had informed us of the incident, I took her down to meet with a detective on the case in the hope that she could identify this man in a photo lineup. Unfortunately, she was not able to do so—maybe because she was only six years old when the incident happened, and the photo may have been even older or perhaps newer. Nevertheless, she was unsuccessful in identifying this individual, and so the case was dropped. Imagine her state of mind now. It is no wonder that every time we go to the mall or a crowded public place, she has a mental breakdown. She still has difficulty expressing her feelings due to lack of trust in adults.

On the other hand, our middle child has always been approved for 100 percent of any kind of psychological care because she was taught how to manipulate people by some of her biological family members at an early age. We learned this from a combination of the information in her social summary packet and information from her older sister. Once our oldest daughter began talking, a lot more truths came out.

I'm baffled as to why a mental-health professional would ask three siblings at the same time in the same room if they had been sexually molested by a certain individual. Please keep in mind that our middle child was always in control of the other two and maintained that control until she came to live with us. If *she* said yes, then of course the other two would follow suit, because they did not want to cross her. This same mental-health provider actually stated in her notes that the alleged sexual abuse and other horrific incidents that our middle child was subjected to when she lived with her birth mother were agreed to be true by two biological family members who were not blood related to the girls' mother.

We discovered later that there had been a great deal of animosity between our girls' birth mother and their paternal family members. The paternal family manipulated our daughter into believing these accusations were true. Later, however, she recanted her story, actually admitting that she was told to go along with it in order to get back at her birth mother for abandoning her and her siblings.

We could never understand how our middle child was diagnosed with all of these disorders, yet nobody felt the need to medicate her in order to control the outbursts she had on a regular basis. This was not an isolated incident; I have seen many other foster children treated this way, all while the foster parents continue to complain about their behaviors. When foster children are initially denied mental-health services and then get approved for only a minimum number of hours, this affects both them and the foster parents, who are ultimately forced to deal with the same behaviors.

With a sibling group, it is hard to believe that some psychologists will charge the state the maximum amount of approved hours per child but see all of the children together in half the time they are being paid for. This goes for any other medical or dental providers where you sit in the waiting room for hours only to have them do a "quickie" once over with the child, barely giving you a chance to even ask questions.

Foster parents are expected to provide a safe environment for their foster children and to protect them from harm. Yet the very system that places children in these homes neglects to provide the additional care the children need to deal with the trauma of being away from their natural parents and acclimating in an unfamiliar home with strangers. All children in foster care need some form of mental-health counseling, in my opinion, especially since they are all diagnosed with PTSD and understandably so. It does not make a lot of sense that children are being denied services because someone in his or her infinite wisdom does not see the need. Even if the child is initially denied and then approved after the case plan was resubmitted with some minor changes, the disruption of services could set a child back for months.

PSR workers are used as glorified babysitters who in some cases spend up to six hours per day for three or four days a week with a foster child, based on the child's case-plan requirements. Prior to the girls being placed in our home, we were told by several people that our children's PSR worker would pick them up from school, take them to their doctor appointments, help them with their homework, and even take them to eat at McDonald's, since they usually have them until close to bedtime or afterward. We could never understand why foster parents would want their PSR worker to take their foster children to doctor appointments, especially mental-health appointments. How can you benefit from your foster children's progress if you are not participating in their mental-health therapy? How can PSR workers manage a child's behavior in the home when they spend their entire session with the child outside of the home? Our children have been through a total of six PSR workers in the last three years—three since they have been with us—and we haven't seen any significant changes in the behaviors thus far.

Treatment centers are a joke here in Clark County. The psychiatric treatment centers are designed to treat children and adolescents for a wide range of mental disorders, including different mood disorders and even substance abuse. One of our daughters was an inpatient there for a week. Before she was admitted, she had never wet herself or the bed. Since her release from this inpatient treatment center, she has bedwetting episodes two to three times a week, and she is nine years old! There has not been much of an improvement in her behaviors. In fact, in some ways, they seem to have gotten worse. She tried unsuccessfully to kill one of our dogs by hitting the dog with a clipboard because she said that the dog's barking was annoying to her. Her anger is out of control most of the time.

We believe this change in behavior was a way to elicit sympathy from the counselors, and she used her well-honed manipulation and acting skills to garner sympathy for herself. Once she was able to get this from the counselors, all bets were off. She refused to participate in the sessions, as she said her feelings were getting hurt and she didn't want to. They allowed her to not participate and fed into her manipulating ways. This is a nine-year-old girl playing games with a supposedly well-trained and well-educated mental-health counseling staff. They should have been able to see through this, especially since we warned them when she was admitted and that was the reason we brought her there.

Once she was released and came back home, the sympathy and coddling ceased, and she started to act out because her ploys were not working any longer. She has repeatedly said she wants to go back to inpatient, and one time she even said she wanted one of her counselors to be her new mother. This would not be an expected result of a stay in a professional mental-health treatment facility.

Ironically, we wanted to place her in a treatment center a little over a year before the time when she actually did go, but we couldn't because we were told by her caseworker that since she was still a foster child, we were not permitted to separate her from her siblings. Imagine our surprise later when we began fostering other children and found out that there were many siblings who are separated because of one being in an inpatient treatment facility.

Preventing children from receiving proper inpatient medical treatment with the excuse of keeping them in a foster home together with their siblings is directly impeding their treatment progress. The system is broken, and the children are the ones who are suffering. If foster children cannot acquire the appropriate psychological services, they may exhibit more aggressive behaviors in the home, which in turn can lead to serious challenges for the foster parents. Ultimately, situations like these have culminated in child abuse and neglect.

During your experience as foster and/or adoptive parents, you will undoubtedly hear about the many failed placements and adoptions of foster children, followed by the phrase, "by no fault of their own."

Truthfully it is not the children's fault, but neither is it the foster parent's fault. Whose fault is it? The foster-care system, in my opinion, must accept the blame.

Families who adopt children with special needs receive adoption subsidies, yet much-needed medical and psychological services are not easily obtainable or too costly, or the parents are given little to no information as to where to go for these types of services. Part of the adoption subsidy includes Medicaid health insurance for the children until they reach the age of eighteen, but not every physician's office accepts Medicaid. Consequently, if you don't have any other insurance, the services that are available to your children—particularly services with a specialist like a pediatric urologist or gastroenterologist—are limited. Referrals from the pediatrician to a specialty provider come with certain requirements that need to be followed before a referral is made. This can be quite frustrating, and to some foster parents, it is not worth the struggle and headache to deal with until the child turns eighteen years old. Therefore, they decide against adoption.

The training requirements to be a foster or adoptive parent in Clark County, do include additional training classes for parents who may be interested in fostering to adopt. Unfortunately, it is not mandatory to attend these classes, and it should be. If there are additional services available for foster parents who have children with medical special needs, the county should encourage parents to seek out all available options for these children, not just send class schedules and information flyers in the mail. If there is not enough support or services available, foster parents need to go after the welfare system to obtain this much-needed medical care. Foster and adopted children on Medicaid should *never* be denied medical services of any kind. This lack of support will only result in more failed adoptions, because foster parents will not feel that it is worth the trouble, and why should they?

Two of our children are currently under the care of a pediatric endocrinologist and will continue to see a specialist for the rest of their lives. Sadly for us, this specialist does not take Medicaid. Therefore, we must use our insurance and pay the required co-pays, or find another specialist that does accept Medicaid. In the long run, the children are the ones who lose. If the state does not work with adoptive and foster parents to ensure that children with special needs are receiving the maximum services needed, there will continue to be adoption dissolutions and placement disruptions. Foster and adopted children will continue to be abused and neglected, and the system will have again failed them.

Some will say that when you adopt these children, you are on your own, and why should you receive any help or subsidy at all? But the subsidies are a bargain compared to the cost of keeping these children in state foster care until they are eighteen years old—and that's not to mention the cost in the emotional well-being of the children, who would have no stability or place to call home. Growing up in the system is not the type of environment we are trying to create for the very people we are attempting to protect by removing them for whatever reason from their biological homes.

The biggest benefit to subsidizing adoptions is the very reason there is a foster system to begin with, and that is to provide for the safety and well-being of the children. Subsidizing that should not ever be a question in anyone's mind. Adoption also prevents children from being termed out of foster care and dumped in the streets to fend for themselves. What do you think the outcome of that will be? We will be paying incarceration costs and creating more criminals for our society to deal with.

Chapter 8

Mental-Health Needs of Foster Children

Imagine you're looking for a new vehicle. You've narrowed the field down to a few styles and features that you desire. You start visiting dealerships to compare the various makes and models. After comparing, reading, and possibly taking a test drive, you make the decision to purchase a certain vehicle that you feel meets all your criteria. At first, everything is just as you expected. The vehicle runs great. It's very comfortable to drive, and the family is thrilled with the ride.

Then you start to notice little things, like the slight vibration that creeps in at freeway speeds and the air-conditioning that will not maintain cool temperatures when the vehicle is stopped at a traffic light or the temperature outside is over ninety degrees. Nothing unbearable, just minor annoyances.

More of these minor issues come up in the next few months, but nothing that makes you think you may have a lemon. You contact the dealer, and he assures you that a few problems are to be expected with any new vehicle purchased, and everything should be okay from now on. And indeed, the next few months go by with very few problems. You notice little things that just don't seem quite 100 percent right, but you think maybe you're just looking for problems and are being overly sensitive. Overall, you're happy with the purchase and have no regrets.

Then it happens. One day as you are traveling down the freeway, you start to hear a horrible noise coming from the engine compartment. You check the gauges and everything seems normal, but it is getting worse, and you decide to pull over and investigate. When you open the hood, you see the problem. The cooling fans have broken, and the brackets holding the fan assembly to the radiator have cracked. You think it's no big deal and call roadside assistance to tow you to the dealer for repair.

After all, it's under warranty, and the work won't cost anything. You should be all fixed by the end of the day.

Instead, things quickly go downhill. While the car is at the dealer, the mechanic discovers an unknown issue and calls the manufacturer about it. The manufacturer tells the dealer to take the car to a specialist and get it analyzed. It seems there was a problem with the assembly at the factory, but the dealer promises to get it repaired by the next day, and that should be the end of your problems.

At this point, you are slightly annoyed at the inconvenience, but the dealer gives you a loaner vehicle to use, and you go home. Doubts about the purchase start to surface, and you wonder if you may have a lemon. The next day, the dealer calls to say the mechanic repaired all the problems, everything is in tip-top condition, and all the problems are repaired. Everything seems fine for several weeks . . . until another noise and vibration starts. This time, without warning, all hell breaks loose. The driveshaft separates from the rear end, and you are barely able to get the vehicle off the road without a serious crash occurring.

This time, the dealer offers to replace your vehicle with another one. After checking on inventory, he informs you that it will take several weeks to get a replacement with the same options and accessories you had on your first vehicle. You're offered a loaner, and you drive away. In a few weeks, your new vehicle arrives, and after the paperwork is complete, you take it home. This time you have no problems, and although there is always that feeling that something is going to happen at any moment, nothing does.

If only things were this simple when dealing with foster children or, especially, adopted children! We have seen this situation play out in our personal experience. Fortunately, the foster placements have given us very few unmanageable problems—only the typical behavior issues for the age of the placement and what would be expected from children displaced suddenly from their home. So far, there have been no driveshaft separations or even minor noises or vibrations. The three children we adopted, however, are another story entirely.

When we are called for a foster placement and we have the available room, we will talk to the former foster parents (if we are taking them from another placement) or meet the children at the holding facility to see how they interact with us and if they will be a good fit in our home. As we will only take long-term placements, this is crucial to the success of the placement. We have usually only taken placements that have previously been placed and the former foster parents cannot continue care for one reason or another, usually because the placement ended up being for longer than anticipated. This works out great for us and also lets us have a little history on behaviors and issues that have been found. It also prevents a placement from happening that would not work out and further disrupting the children. Additionally, it allows us to prepare for any special needs that may be present, such as eating disorders, sleeping problems, allergies, or other medical needs. We can have a look at what the medical history is and see what has been entered into the social summary as far as what the counseling services, if any, have found.

This is similar to buying a used car from someone who has driven it for a while and is willing to tell you all the little quirks, idiosyncrasies, and problems they have experienced. You know exactly what you are getting and what to expect. I would like to think this is one of the many reasons we have had successful placements.

There is one outlet available if things should not work out, and that is giving a ten-day notice because we cannot care for this placement. That gives the placement team time to find another home that would be suitable. When you accept a placement, you are required to keep the children for ten days under the terms of your foster license agreement. I do not necessarily agree with this, as it can cause extreme stress or worse if the placement is unmanageable. This could be the stressor that causes a foster parent to crack and potentially harm a child. At the same time, if the home is somewhat stable, it may be the best place for a tough placement to be until the placement team can find a home that can deal with the behavior and provide the type of care that is needed.

As in the analogy of buying a new car, there is always the chance that things will go along just fine until there is a breakdown. Just as with the car, there is no way to predict when or if this may happen. When it does, it usually will catch you so off guard that you can't believe what just happened. It is at this time that a call to the dealer is in order—or in this case, the caseworker—to see about remedying the situation. Usually that will involve a whole series of workers assigned to diagnose the problem and get the child into therapy. Along with this comes some sort of medication to "calm them down" and make the child docile.

Medication may or may not be the right solution, but it is the one that is prescribed in most cases. The system is only interested in finding a warehouse to keep the children, and if that means medicating them so they can stay in a placement, as unfortunate as it may sound that is what will happen. Imagine, then, what chaos ensues when the child is either returned to the natural parents or adopted, and the parents decide they do not want the child medicated. At this point, parents will be bombarded with behaviors they did not plan on or expect.

The social summary and medical packet that comes with each child is supposed to detail all of this. Usually it will state that the child is on medication or is being treated for some disorder of the day, but rarely will it explain in plain English what that means in terms of daily behavior. The doctors who are seeing these children are contracted with the state to provide services to foster children. Most of them will not see any patients outside of state care or Medicaid. They have to justify their existence and necessity by finding disorders, either real or imaginary, that these children have and then get them on the hamster wheel of continual treatment and visits.

I have heard the most bizarre and crazy terms for disorders that these children have. There is more alphabet soup for these disorders than there are suffixes behind the names of those who "treat" them. The amazing thing is that these disorders can only be treated by repeated visits to a psychiatrist or other provider. Usually, these visits consist of briefly asking how things are, taking a few notes, and then refilling and/or adjusting the medication.

I do not fault the providers for what they do. This is how they were taught, and when it comes right down to it, they are not miracle workers. Like any medical professionals, they can only do what they were taught and what the current literature suggests for treatment. Also, most foster parents are looking for a magic pill or something that will keep these children from acting out. I can tell you from personal experience that there is no such thing. These children were traumatized for the most part during their formative years, and there is no pill that is going to reverse that. Only with years of rebuilding and gaining trust will these disorders tend to get better. I do not dispute that medication can make things much more bearable within the home; however, as we found from firsthand dealings, the drugs come with the price of side effects.

The most commonly used drugs are Risperdal, Abilify, Seroquel, and Zyprexa. These drugs are classified as mood-altering drugs, and Risperdal in itself is the subject of extensive litigation. One of our adopted daughters was on this drug for a period of time, and it caused her to become very loopy. At the same time, she was being seen by other doctors for other medical issues, and we were having regular blood work done for monitoring another disease. Her thyroid went from normal to abnormal during the time she was on this medicine. Now she has thyroid disease and is on thyroid medication for low thyroid function, and will be for the rest of her life. She has also developed psoriasis. Since she was taken off the medication, the skin problem cleared up for the most part, but the thyroid problem is permanent.

Incidentally, we were never told by her psychiatrist that she would need to be weaned off her antipsychotic drugs gradually to possibly prevent some of these side effects. This is an example of the things that are not disclosed to you when you sign up for foster parenting. There is no way for the caseworkers to know that this will happen. The issue is that these children were in foster care for almost three years prior to us adopting them, and nothing was ever found in that time about their medical issues. We found out more about medical and psychological issues in the three months after we adopted them than the state and the former foster parents ever bothered to find out.

Each girl came to us with a social summary that was supposed to tell us about any medical, developmental, and behavior issues. This would be great if they had been taken to doctors and providers who truly cared and bothered to diagnose what was wrong. Nothing that we were able to find out in three months after we adopted them was ever mentioned by anyone prior to the adoption. Either it was known and was withheld from us, or—as we believe is the case—they were never taken to anyone who cared enough to take the time to find out what was wrong. This is a prime example of children being placed in homes for the purpose of warehousing until such time they can either be adopted out of the system or successfully placed in a permanent foster home that will take care of them until they are eighteen and term out. The children are taken in for their required medical, dental, and vision visits, and a bare minimum standard of care is upheld. When looking at the overall picture, it is no surprise that these children come with extreme baggage. This results in multiple failed adoptions and permanency in the foster system. Each time a home is changed, it adds to the damage being done to the children.

In previous chapters, I've mentioned reactive attachment disorder, or RAD. This is disorder is fairly prevalent among foster children, and we were actually told by our children's caseworker that one of our children has it. RAD is caused by a lack of trust in people from being abandoned at a young age, usually by the birth mother, as well as a lack of bonding with the mother. The behaviors that result from this disorder are beyond what can be written about in one chapter or even ten. There are many excellent books discussing this disorder, such as *When Love Is Not Enough: A Guide to Parenting Children with RAD* by Nancy Thomas, *Broken Spirits—Lost Souls: Loving Children with Attachment and Bonding Difficulties* by Jane E. Ryan, and *Attaching in Adoption: Practical Tools for Today's Parents* by Deborah D. Gray. These are just of few books that describe in exacting detail the damage it causes to both the children who suffer from it and the families they tear apart. These books are definitely worth reading if you are considering adopting or fostering children who have been or are diagnosed with RAD. They outline what can be expected in the worst cases of children being traumatized and also explain the bizarre behaviors in those who only have a mild case of this disorder. These books do a very good job of explaining why many adoptions fail. Unless you have a child with this disorder living with you, as we do, explaining these behaviors to others is always met with dis-belief. Anyone who has not been through this can even begin to understand what it is like. This is one reason many children are permanently bound into the foster care system as they cannot understand what is going on with these children when they are placed with them. Adoptions in most of these cases fail for this reason. An adoptive family sees this behavior and cannot cope with it, as it is so incredibly bizarre.

The impact of RAD was downplayed considerably when we were going through the adoption process; we had no idea what was in store for us. One of the most frightening things about this disorder is that the children who have it are manipulative, know how to play the system, and can turn it off and on at will. Our daughter with RAD showed none of the symptoms we are living with now during the six months we fostered her and her sisters prior to adoption. Once the adoption was final, the behavior started getting worse almost as soon as we got home from the courthouse. This caught us off guard, and we have been battling it ever since.

We are convinced that if the foster-care system were set up the way I have discussed, this would not have been the problem it has become. She would have been diagnosed and put in a treatment facility or intense-care home that deals with these disorders a long time ago. We would have been made aware of what we were getting into, as the social summaries would have spelled this out. The problem is that the system has no incentive to treat and/or disclose these problems; doing so runs counter to the goal of placing as many children as possible. If the real issues were disclosed to prospective adoptive parents, there would be a lot fewer adoptions. This is a tough issue to resolve, as the most obvious alternative would be to institutionalize these children or place them in high-maintenance therapeutic foster homes until they learn how to cope in society.

RAD is on the extreme end of the spectrum of issues that may be discovered once children are placed in foster or adoptive homes. Other issues include medical conditions and learning disabilities. These are not as difficult to deal with as behavior problems, because they are usually easier to accurately diagnose and treat. With behavioral problems and disorders, it can be very hard to determine what the cause is, as the disorder can be either psychological or caused by fetal alcohol syndrome, drug use by the mother while pregnant, or a physical injury caused by abuse while in the womb. This is usually not known, as the true history of children in foster care is rarely provided. Our children, for example, were abandoned by their birth mother, and their other biological family members did not want them. There were no accurate birth records and no records of medical care until they were placed in the system. There was also no information known about the birth father, as he was deported and imprisoned.

It may seem as though I am being very hard on the system and its workers. I will not make any apologies for this, and I will stand behind every comment I have made throughout this book. In the course of our involvement with the foster system, we have had the privilege of working with some very dedicated and hardworking caseworkers. They have proven they are truly in it for the benefit of the children. Unfortunately, they are too few and far between. The experience of other foster parents I have spoken with about this are also mixed. If the caseworkers don't do their jobs as they are supposed to, the whole system fails the very people it is supposed to protect.

Everyone involved in foster care and foster-to-adopt has to remember that the most important reason we do what we do is for the children. I have mentioned many times before that the children did not have a choice about their situation and what has happened to them. Regardless of what they may do, it must be remembered that they are reacting to and expressing their sadness, confusion, and anger in the only way they know how. They have not been taught the proper coping skills, and in many cases were too busy worrying about where their next meal was coming from or where they were going to sleep that night to understand that they were not being taken care of the way they should have been. When placed in a setting where those issues are not a concern, they will finally express their anger, because they can now see how they should have been living. They will wonder why they did not have this in their natural parent's home, and they will misdirect their rage at the current parent. This is where a great deal of patience and understanding is required to understand the feelings and emotions that are overwhelming them.

It is unfortunate that all this is so blatantly overlooked from within the system. The caseworkers and the state itself do not see the need for the type of treatment these children so desperately require. There are neither enough mental-health facilities nor any provisions for sending children to a facility if the behavior warrants it. There is a compelling need for treatment beyond outpatient visits with psychiatrists and psychologists, as well as the general BST/PSR workers who are so commonly sent to meet with these children.

When that treatment is not provided, the foster parents are left to pay the consequences, in many instances with no help and no idea where to turn. While it is no secret that both state and federal budgets are generally bankrupt, it is our belief that those who do not have the resources should not have to suffer any further than they already have. This would be the children. The natural parents are able to get welfare, food stamps, counseling, and housing assistance, while the children are not able to get the help they need to cope with both the displacement from their natural home and the feelings of anger and confusion from being placed in a strange home with strange people. This seems like a miscarriage of justice.

How should this issue be addressed? This is a huge problem that will not and cannot be solved overnight. The first step would be recognition that there is a problem that needs to be addressed. This would have to come from foster parents raising awareness with county and state workers. Next would be those same workers implementing awareness at the case level and bringing those findings to the agencies for action. This is not going to be an overnight process, but it is something that needs to be started immediately.

The next portion of this chapter provides some details of our experiences with the mental-health system in Clark County, as well as the experiences of a former foster parent from another state who had a similar experience to ours several years ago.

In Clark County, there are two major mental-health facilities that deal with adolescents. One of our daughters was a resident of one of those facilities for one week, yet she came out acting even worse than before she went in. This is the daughter who has been diagnosed with severe RAD and bipolar disorder. After multiple instances of lying about things that happened to her that triggered several CPS investigations, we placed her in the facility to get help for her problems. After one week, I received a call at my job from the facility that I needed to come get her right now. Not after work or later that day—right now. They were no longer willing or able to work with her, as she refused to participate in any group sessions, made allegations against a five-year-old boy she said threatened to kill her, and in general caused a disturbance in the facility. These, of course, were the very reasons she was sent there to begin with.

This facility had been recommended and referred by the psychiatrist who was treating her. This is known as the best treatment center in Las Vegas. It is a sad testimony to the mental-health system that they are not able to treat an eight-year-old because she was combative and uncooperative the entire time. These workers are supposedly trained to work with children who have the types of disorders that our daughter has, and they were not even able to maintain that professionalism with her for one week! This is the level of mental-health care that is currently available.

Since this episode, we have been dealing with the disruptive behaviors in our household and are currently looking for an out-of-state facility that will take our child in. Unfortunately, there are very few facilities across the country that will take in children this young.

Most have a minimum age requirement of twelve. Where does that leave children who need help at a younger age? Making them wait until they turn twelve only serves to ingrain the problems much deeper and causes undue stress and hardship for the parents, the siblings, and the children themselves.

As I mentioned earlier, here in Clark County, children must be fostered for a minimum of six months prior to adoption so that the prospective parents have some time to get to know the children and their behaviors, and the children have time to adjust to their new home. In many instances, the children are able to maintain relatively normal behaviors for that period of time; however, in our case, some of the behaviors came out right away as soon as our children were placed with us. Unfortunately, they were blatantly blown off by the caseworkers as a natural phase of adjustment to a new home. Being new to the system, we did not know better. A word of advice from our experience: do your due diligence prior to making any final decisions when fostering to adopt. It is much better to terminate an adoption prior to it being finalized than to suffer with children who will not act like "normal" children once they become a part of your family—or something much worse that could possibly end tragically.

In our case, we decided to adopt this sibling group of three sisters who seemed to be somewhat well adjusted, even though there were signs that there might be some issues. We thought at first it was all part of the adjustment process. After the fact, we started to discover that these behaviors were much more prevalent and ingrained than we thought. Had we researched the state rules and regulations on the process of fostering to adopt and known what our rights were, and maybe reached out to other parents who adopted in the same way, we would have known what to expect and how to better handle the behaviors as they surfaced. This is another reason to require more training for potential adoptive parents and foster parents of children with special needs. Additionally, a support group that focuses on foster parents who deal with these very issues or something similar could make the transition a little easier.

We love our children, and they are ours; however, if we had better knowledge of what to expect, it is likely that we would not have made the decision to adopt them at that time. We would have definitely demanded more time before finalizing the adoption. It is important for anyone to have that ability to make an informed decision. In no way are we insinuating the children are to blame in any way for the way they were treated and placed in the foster system. We are advocating for these children to receive the help that they need.

Another foster family we have come to know has had similar experiences with the system in another state. They adopted a sibling group some years ago, and although the children have all grown up now, even as adults they still show signs of trauma stemming from their childhood abuse and neglect. The children—two girls and one boy—were eight, twelve, and thirteen at the time they were adopted. They had already been through three failed adoptions and obviously came with some baggage and issues. Mostly these were anger issues and acting out on this anger.

The foster parents sent their two daughters to a private Christian therapeutic boarding school in Texas for girls with behavioral issues, at their own expense. The oldest daughter went for one year at the age of thirteen and then again at seventeen, but the second time for only two weeks, as she was withdrawn by her biological mother. This child had been molested for six years by a former foster parent, which caused much of the anger she was exhibiting. Her sister went to a different Christian boarding school for nine months and then returned home. The younger sister and brother both have good well-adjusted lives today. The older daughter however, has not been so fortunate; she turned to drugs and married an abusive man she met while in jail. She currently has three children, all under the age of four years, and is expecting a fourth one in a few months.

The ironic twist to this is that her children were taken away from her and placed in our care. Unfortunately, these children will be returning home soon because of a failed court system that feels children in foster care should be allowed to return home to their biological parents while the parents work on their "case plan." All this particular mother had to do was promise to stay away from their abusive father (who, by the way, she depends on financially), submit to random drug tests, and attend parenting classes while her children are allowed to live with her and her mother-in-law. It is unfortunate that this will result in more statistics about harm coming to children through the foster-care system.

We have become close with the children's maternal grandparents, and the grandmother has shared her experiences with us regarding her adopted children. She has said that sending their daughters to a

Christian behavioral boarding school did make a difference, but that the oldest (whose children we fostered) needed more time and care to get through her issues. If this couple had received financial support from the state, their daughter would have been able to stay as long as necessary to help her through her problems; instead, they were forced to withdraw her from the school until they were able to save enough money to reenroll her. Maybe the outcome would have been different. Instead, their grandchildren are inevitably heading down the same path as their daughter has.

Now we try to find a solution as to what can be done to help these children work through their issues and get the help they need. In our case, we went through several psychiatrists for our middle daughter. In one office, we were asked to leave and not come back, as the doctor did not feel he could do anything with her when her behavior became so bad in his office that the other patients were getting upset. Her one-week inpatient stay in the short-term mental-health facility failed for similar reasons. This left us with only one option to address her aggressive behaviors with intensive treatment: a long-term mental-health treatment facility for children and adolescents. Unfortunately, these are very few and far between, and most health-insurance companies—including Medicaid—will not cover them if they are out of state.

We believe there should be long-term child and adolescent facilities available in every state to accommodate the many children who are in need of intense mental-health care. If we look at the homeless population, we find rampant cases of mental illness. While some of this is self-inflicted through drug and alcohol abuse, you have to look at what triggered the substance abuse. Do you think it could be untreated childhood mental-health issues like the ones we've been discussing? If these people had received the help they needed at a young age, could their problems later in life have been mitigated? The small cost of helping these people would be more than offset by the savings in welfare costs, health-care costs, and crimes not committed. Wouldn't it make more sense to spend the time and resources on intervention for children and adolescents instead of reactionary treatments and incarceration for adults?

Our daughter was medicated for a period of time, yet it didn't do anything for her but create more health problems on top of the ones she already has. In her case, medication is not the answer, but I know of many other cases where there is truly an imbalance in brain chemistry that can be maintained by the proper types and doses of certain medications. The problem arises when these people must take medications and attend regular office visits to regulate the dosage. We have seen firsthand that doctors are quick to prescribe a pill that is supposed to stabilize behaviors but actually either just zones the child out or makes him or her become withdrawn and somewhat in a zombie-like state.

If people are found to have a mental illness that is treatable by medication, how do you assure they stay on that medication and actually take it? At what point do they become a danger to either themselves or others sufficient to compel them to take their medication? If adults are put on an antipsychotic drug, they should be monitored as an inpatient to ensure that they maintain a regular regimen, so as not to create an imbalance in the brain because they just simply decide not to take it anymore. I also believe that medication alone is not the answer and that parallel counseling is needed to truly stabilize mental illness. This intensive form of treatment, in my opinion, is beyond the scope of a short-term mental-health treatment facility.

The question then becomes, what do we do with people who at a young age show signs of mental illness? Do we just shrug it off as adolescent behavior and think they will outgrow it, or do we have them analyzed for mental-health issues? We must determine if they pose a threat to anyone including themselves—who will make that determination, and at what point do we say they are not safe to be in society? Do we use the excuse as parents that our children are too much for us to handle and have them committed as a convenience so we don't have to deal with their bad behavior? These are all very serious and troubling questions that have to be addressed for any type of mental-health reform to take place. It is neither a simple nor an easy issue. I certainly do not know the answers to all of these questions, but I also know that the present system does not work and has led to many avoidable incidents, had the perpetrators gotten the help they needed prior to pleading "not guilty by reason of mental defect."

There should be a system in place in every state to treat people with behavioral problems while they are young enough for it to make a difference. At the present time, there are only warehousing facilities that "medicate and vacate" without treating the real problem inside.

Medication is needed in many instances, but that is not the only available treatment that is needed or available. Facilities must be built to take in the patients who are not being helped and have mental-health issues that are beyond the scope of care an outpatient treatment facility can accommodate. No parent likes to admit that he or she has a child with a mental illness and then send that child away for treatment. But sometimes it's the only thing that will help.

I would rather send my child to a long-term treatment facility out-of-state for as long as necessary than give up on her and place her back into the system where she will become even more damaged than before. We must be willing to admit that there is a problem, get out of denial, and take the action necessary to correct the problem. In the case of foster children, this should be something that the state provides as a service, just like the countless BST, PSR, and other workers who in our experience have been nothing but a waste of time and money. If the money that is wasted on these workers—once it is found that they are making no progress—was spent on treatment in an inpatient facility for those cases not treatable on an outpatient basis, I would be willing to bet the overall cost would be less than the current system, and there would be measurably better results in treatment success rates.

Some short-term treatment centers will take children as young as four years old; however, I believe that any type of long-term treatment facility should have a minimum age of eight for commitment. This would obviously have to be on a case-by-case basis. Children ages four through seven would continue to receive outpatient treatment, and if there was no improvement by the age of eight, they can and should go long-term. In the case of our children, they received treatment from a variety of BST and PSR workers as well as psychiatrists and psychologists prior to being placed with us, and all of them stated in their medical documents that there was no improvement in their progress. Had we known to study these reports in-depth, we would have picked up on it. Unfortunately, we were told that they had been showing a significant degree of progress. Shortly after our children were placed in our home, we were able to observe the behaviors more prominently.

We decided to find an outpatient treatment facility where the PSR/BST workers, as well as the psychologist, would actually come into our home for sessions. This worked out quite well in the beginning, as they were able to address the behaviors immediately as they were happening.

This lasted until the PSR worker suggested I put diapers on our then seven-, eight-, and nine-year-olds when we took them to Disney World for *my* peace of mind, as she put it. Imagine their state of mind, walking around a park as big as Disney World with a diaper on at their age! We would be adding humiliation to their already fragile mental state. In retrospect, we had failed yet again with outpatient mental-health care. It was at this point that a long-term treatment solution should have started. It was during this time that we tried the treatment center, which also failed.

We are convinced, based on our personal experiences as well as our discussions with other foster parents, that there is a definite need for complete reform in the mental-health-care system for children. It is the birth parents who are the ones responsible for the children being in foster care to begin with, yet they have a multitude of services and counseling available to them. The children are the ones who suffer from lack of services. Only by raising awareness of this problem and educating our policy makers about these issues and their consequences will any change occur.

Chapter 9

Patience Is a Virtue While Raising Foster or Adopted Children

When friends, families, and even strangers hear of our adoption experience and some of the issues that even today we still struggle with, we usually get mixed responses. I have had people tell us how wonderful it is for us to take in these children and give them a second chance, some even through tears of commiseration expressing their heartfelt approval. There are others, however, who simply ask "Why?" They wonder what we could possibly be thinking at our age. Why would we take in three additional children after all of our biological children have grown up and gone? We are essentially starting all over again.

In the years since our girls first came into our home, we have seen behaviors fluctuate from improvement to regression. We second-guess ourselves at times because we are dumbfounded by some of the devious and conniving things they are capable of doing. It goes without saying that patience diminishes with age; I know that I do not have the patience now that I had when my own children were young. I feel blessed that God has allowed me to maintain the patience that I still have left, but I now understand why most countries have age requirements for parents adopting internationally. There are varying age requirements depending on the country, ranging from no age restrictions in very few countries to no more than fifty-five years' difference between the child and the youngest parent. The common theme is that there must be a minimum age difference of sixteen years between the youngest parent and the child. Here in the United States, there is no age requirement (within reason) as long as the prospective foster/adoptive parents are in reasonably good physical and mental health.

I raised my children to be respectful to us as well as to others, especially other adults. They were taught to respond to their elders with "Yes, sir" and "Yes, ma'am," which they still do today as adults. We always followed the golden rule of "Do unto others as you would have them do unto you." This remains a standard rule in our home. Unfortunately, foster children come from a different background than we as foster parents are normally accustomed to. I have never had any of my biological children tell me to shut up, call me names (at least not to my face), or hit me. I have had all of these things done to me by a foster child, and even one of my own adopted children.

If patience is not mediated as an important trait for foster or adoptive parents, foster children will continue to be at the mercy of their caretakers. It is a known fact that parents, no matter what the age, have more patience with their own children than they do with others'. Our children know their limits with us. Foster children, on the other hand, know what limits we are bound by when disciplining them. I cannot count how many times a parent has received a daggered stare or rude comment for allowing a child to act out uncontrollably in a store. Most foster children are old enough to know better, which is probably what brings the stares and comments. It is quite unnerving to see an eight-, nine-, or even ten-year-old child throw a tantrum in the middle of a store or even a shopping mall. I have heard loud comments like, "All they need is an old-fashioned butt spanking!" What the child knows that all those onlookers do not are the regulations against imposing that kind of discipline on a foster child.

Of course, there are ways to discipline a child that do not involve spanking. A combination of disciplining tactics can be utilized on a child that does not include hitting or humiliating. Each time we would put one of our adopted daughters in time-out, she would scream, cuss, bang the walls with her head, and talk filthy. I used to turn on our vacuum cleaner and put it in front of the door of the room that she was in time-out in, so nobody could hear her until her time was up. Her therapist told us that the next time we put her in time-out, we should let her know that she would stay there until she stopped talking and quit banging her head on the wall. Only then would her time-out start. If she began to do any of the things mentioned above during her time-out, then her time would start all over again until she finally decided to stop. Believe it or not, this strategy actually worked, and still does. It may not work for everyone, but the idea is to utilize age-appropriate disciplinary measures.

Time-out is pretty much the only discipline allowed when it comes to foster children. Unfortunately for foster parents, the children who know this the best will ultimately behave the worst. Older children can be given extra chores or have privileges like phones or laptops taken away as a punishment for misbehaving, but this too can result in disaster. I have read some horrific stories about foster and adopted children's behaviors from former foster mothers who are currently serving prison time for their foster children's deaths.

I do not condone any physical abuse to a child regardless of behavior. In the case of Shameeka Davis, who took in her twin niece and nephew and cared for them under the foster-care system until her niece's death at the hands of Shameeka herself, the Department of Human Services reports that she was complaining of being overwhelmed years before. This shows that even a relative placement does not automatically mean the children will be safe and taken care of properly, nor does it mean that they will not be abused. Those children were born to a drug-addicted mother, so they were undoubtedly going to exhibit long-term aftereffects from in utero drug exposure. This woman should have never been allowed to take these children without proper training on how to handle drug-born babies.

A person's age does not always play a part in how well he or she can handle certain behaviors. Patience, however, does. When we are asked if we can take a foster child in our home, we always request as much of a history on the child as possible, including behaviors and sleeping and eating habits. I will not take a baby long-term who does not sleep all night, because we usually do not go to bed until around midnight to sometimes 2:00am. We currently have a total of seven children in our home (four of them fosters) who do sleep all night, but are up by seven. I will admit that I do not like my sleep interrupted during the night on a regular basis, so I would not allow myself to be placed in a situation where I could potentially lose control.

During foster-training classes, potential foster parents are given a questionnaire on the ages and type of children they would be willing to take into their home. This, I am sure, is placed in our records and then sent to the DFS placement team. Unfortunately for most of us, our situation changes from time to time, which can result in requesting a change in the age, gender, or even the number of beds your home has available. Because of the likelihood of these changes, foster parents should be given this questionnaire every three months. Instead, updates are not mandated, and foster parents are put in a position of accepting placements they are not physically or emotionally able to handle. Some foster homes will reluctantly accept these placements thinking they are for a very short time, and they end up being long-term. Some actual family members will take children out of a sense of obligation, because the children are related to them. Sadly, as with Shameeka Davis and many others like her, the placement ends tragically.

We all have a finite degree of patience that defines our boundaries with children. There are many happily married couples, as well as single men and women, who do not have any children for this reason. Placing a child in one of these homes could cause a catastrophe—as could accepting children in your home who have more issues than you are prepared to deal with.

Chapter 10

Not in the Best Interest of Anyone

This chapter will look at how the child-welfare system and the courts are working against the very people they are mandated to protect. It will also consider the lack of training and preparation foster parents receive for the issues they will face. Although our adopted daughter is only ten years old at the time of this writing, she has had behavioral issues for as long as she has been in the system. While she was never abused within the system, she was definitely damaged by it, as well as being untreated for disorders that the child-welfare system was aware of. If you are considering adopting children from the foster-care system, the issues raised in this chapter should not be ignored.

When foster children are first introduced into the new home, there is a honeymoon period of a few weeks. During this time, the foster parents are usually not aware of the storm that may be coming. When the adoption becomes final, that's when the real party begins. With our girls, there were multiple episodes of acting out, including rubbing feces on the new bed we had just purchased for them; pouring milk on the new kitchen table we had just bought and ruining the finish; and hitting, kicking, and saying they hated me. These behaviors came about unexpectedly and without any warning. The feelings of rage that this incites are indescribable. It makes it understandable, but in no way justifiable, that foster or adoptive parents sometimes respond with violence toward the children. This is yet another example of why training is needed on what to expect with placements. In our case, our adopted children had been in a therapeutic foster home until they were placed with us for adoption. We were ill-prepared for what that meant.

A therapeutic foster home is a home in which the foster parents have had extensive training and are equipped to handle the special needs of problem children. We did not have such training, and we were not equipped. This placement should not have happened until we were both made fully aware of all the behaviors we might encounter and had taken classes on how to deal with them.

Foster parents receive social summaries that are supposed to detail the issues the children are having and have had. The summaries are also supposed to inform anyone who reads them of the therapies the children are receiving and the progress they are making. We did not know how to read and interpret this document, although it all became painfully clear after the fact. The one thing we learned—and the thing I am forewarning others about—is not to take this document at face value. Read and then reread it several times, as there is always more that seems to be brought out each time it is read. We found many things that were omitted and many inconsistencies in the diagnoses from the many workers who had interacted with these children. Everything in this document needs to be checked out and questioned.

Of course, not every child who comes into the system has known issues and needs, especially if he or she was just removed from the home a few hours ago. This is why the current rule that children can only be kept in state-run holding facilities for twenty-four to forty-eight hours after being removed from their natural home needs to be changed. It puts extreme pressure on placement workers, who must place the child literally overnight in a foster home and hope that it works out. If it does not, then that child is put back in the mix to be placed in a different home, again within the required time limit. So begins an endless cycle of placements, replacements, and on and on. The only good thing about this is that now a little more may be known about the child's behavior, and perhaps the next placement home will be more in line with the child's needs.

As adoptive parents, we have faced many issues with the daughters we adopted out of foster care. As foster parents to children who have been placed with us since then, however, we have not had to deal with any issues. We only take long-term placements, and usually they have been previously placed in a home that was not ready or willing to provide long-term care. When the child comes into our home, we have a very good idea what to expect, as he or she has already been in care for a period of time and most issues have been revealed. Also, we are very specific in our criteria for placement as far as age, gender, and siblings. We are aware of our abilities and limitations and do not go beyond them.

We have been asked many times to take a placement outside of these guidelines, and we have to turn it down. We always feel bad about doing this, but we are aware of what our home can support and what needs we are able to accommodate. We know that going outside our boundaries will be stressful for both our household and the foster child. We are not in this for money and are not interested in filling an available bed so we can get paid, so we are able to say no when necessary.

When we do take in children, the first thing that happens is that we go through everything they have brought with them. Usually this means that our garbage pickup the next week is three bags more than usual. Most of the clothing is either so worn or dirty that it is unusable, or more commonly does not fit. This is especially true of shoes. Most of the toys are so broken that they also have to go. We will go shopping and get the children clothing and shoes that fit, as well as toys that work and are appropriate for the children's ages. Normally, this cash outlay uses up the first month's reimbursement that will come about thirty days later. Most of these children are growing, so this is an ongoing process that does not stop. Trust me when I say that the money we get does not cover everything needed to properly take care of the children. Perhaps our standard of care is higher than most, but we feel that the care these children receive should be no different from the way we would care for our own.

This is another failing that is prevalent throughout the system. While not directly the result of social workers or state workers not caring or doing their jobs, it is an issue that should be addressed at the introductory level and at the initial training sessions. It should also be followed up during subsequent visits while children are in care. It is not very difficult to observe what the children are wearing as well as what they eat and play with. I believe that a part of the training process should be driving home the fact that the reason for having foster homes is to take care of the children and provide for their needs, not to take in the maximum number of kids possible and neglect their needs because the mortgage and the car payment are due.

There is a place in Clark County that offers clothing and a few toys to children who are new to the foster-care system. Each time a child is placed in a home, DFS provides a certificate for three outfits, a pair of shoes, and one toy. All of the items are donated, and most are in acceptable condition. The problem is that in our experience, this is all the child gets. Most foster parents spend the least amount possible to maintain the child, and we do not think that is right.

We occasionally will take a temporary placement to help out foster parents who are going on vacation or who have something coming up that they don't want to or can't take their foster children along for. When this happens, we get paid for the time that we have the children. I can only recall one time where we came away from this without spending more than we got. Usually it went to replace shoes and clothing that were not wearable or did not fit. This reinforces our view that most people are in this for what they think is easy money, and most of these children come from homes where they had very little or nothing and were neglected so they do not know the difference. This is a failing of the caseworkers and the child-welfare department. We feel that these children should be treated just as if they were natural children and deserve to have everything that a "normal" child should have.

Again, this is something that is never talked about in the initial training classes. The child-welfare system is so desperate for foster homes that unless there is a glaring issue with criminal background or an inappropriate housing situation, they will approve the home and begin to place children there. It is sad that there is no emphasis placed on what the children need and that the foster parents are being paid to provide this. While a stable and loving home is very much necessary, so are basics like clothing and good food. The training classes go over the rules and the mechanics of dealing with damaged children, but they do not touch on providing for the children beyond the bare minimum required by the state.

If foster parents are not able to provide the things these children need on their own using the same standards they would if these were their own kids, then the standards of care mandated for foster care should be upgraded. This may eliminate some foster homes, but my feeling is that it would be for the better, as the ones that remained would be in it for the right reasons and with a pure motive of truly providing for the kids. When children are in a home purely for the financial support of the household, how well do you think the foster parents are going to provide for the children? When a need arises for a child that conflicts with paying a household bill, do you think a new pair of shoes, diapers, or food for that child is going to come first? In my opinion, the child is going to do without.

Child-welfare agencies are tasked with overseeing the safety and security of the children under their wing. It is tragic when a child is taken from a home he knows, no matter how bad the conditions are, and told he is going to be taken care of by a new family for a while until his own parents can correct their problems—and then finds himself in just as bad or in some cases a worse situation than where he came from. That is a failing of the child-welfare system that could be easily corrected. It's true that these changes will reduce the number of foster homes available. But isn't it better to have fewer homes if it also means a reduction in the problems in foster homes that there we see today? One abused, neglected, or in the extreme cases murdered child is one too many.

Fewer foster homes would be needed in the first place if the courts didn't prioritize the rights of the birth parents and leave the children in foster-care limbo. Federal guidelines regulate the amount of time a child can be in foster care (eighteen months) until a permanency plan is to be implemented, meaning termination of parental rights and the children either being taken in by a family member or placed for adoption. The intention is to give children a sense of permanency and stability instead of allowing them to be bounced from home to home while the parents continue to party on and decide if they want to straighten up and get their children back. In our years of fostering, we have had only one placement who was reunified successfully with the birth parents. All others have gone to extended family members.

The whole idea of DFS is to protect the child and keep him or her safe. In most cases, being with the parent is not safe for him. The parents are only interested in getting the child returned and will do anything to attain that, most of the time not in true compliance with their case plan. This is why DFS is such a revolving door for children. The courts order the children reunified with total disregard for the safety of the child.

There is an average time of three months between court hearings. In that time, the foster parents have been with the child twenty-four hours a day and the caseworkers have interacted with both the parents and the child. The judge listens to the reports for about twenty minutes and then issues a decision, usually in total disregard of what has been said in the courtroom. I blame the courts above all others for the problems in the child-welfare system. All the other issues discussed contribute to the problem, but the courts are the deciding factor when it comes to permanency for the child.

We have been involved in numerous court hearings, and the judge has always acted without regard for the facts and evidence, or the welfare and safety of the child. In fact, we had our own experience only a few months ago. I testified in court on behalf of three children who were in our care at the time. Our intent was to prove that these children would be better off staying with us until their mother was able to get herself together as opposed to going to the paternal grandmother. The paternal grandmother was granted custody, and the only conditions were that she had to attain a babysitter to assist in the care of the children and be able to pass a criminal background check.

The other terms of this deal were that the birth mother (who was pregnant with her fourth child) would also get to live in the home with her mother-in-law (the paternal grandmother) and the babysitter; however, she could not be left alone with the children. The children's maternal grandmother testified on our behalf, as she was very much aware of the adversarial relationship between her daughter and her daughter's mother-in-law, considering her daughter and grandchildren had been living with her in Oregon for six months until a few months prior to the court hearing. According to the maternal grandmother, her daughter had confided in her regarding the unnatural goings-on in her mother-in-law's home, which included physical and mental abuse to her and her children by both her husband and his mother, and of course her own not-so-stable relationship with her mother-in-law.

The maternal grandmother had called CPS when her daughter decided to suddenly accompany her husband back to Las Vegas with the children in tow. Within hours of her daughter arriving back in Las Vegas, CPS removed the children from their home and placed them in protective custody. These children were placed in our home shortly thereafter. Three weeks from the day we received this placement, the children's maternal grandmother and I testified in court on the children's behalf.

According to the children's maternal grandmother, the children went back to live with their paternal grandmother and birth mother approximately one month after the court hearing. Six weeks after the children were returned home, their mother gave birth to her fourth child. With a new baby to care for, the paternal grandmother decided that her other three grandchildren were no longer worth the trouble, and she dropped them off at the placement center. Apparently the mother and grandmother had been fighting again.

On the third day after the baby was born, the infant was removed from the hospital and taken to the placement center with her other siblings. The two youngest of the four siblings were placed together in a foster home almost immediately; however, the two oldest children weren't so lucky. They stayed at the placement center for more than a month before being placed in a foster home together, but separate from their younger siblings. Almost two weeks after the children had been taken back to the placement center, their paternal grandmother passed away suddenly, and the birth mother has not shown up to any visits or court hearings, nor has she submitted to any of her required drug tests.

Had the judge ordered the children to stay with us, they would all four be in our home today, together, and in continual contact with their maternal grandparents, aunts, and uncles. Instead, they are split up in two foster homes and have minimal phone contact with their maternal grandmother only. Of all the similar experiences we have had with foster children, this one has been the hardest to come to terms with. In the end, the children are the ones who suffer.

This scenario is similar to a crosswalk that is put in after a child is hit by a car on the way to school. Maybe then the courts will revisit the position they have taken and stop the madness of sending children home without considering all the facts of the case that is presented.

Chapter 11

Suggestions for Change

Despite all that has been presented here and even more that has not, I don't want you to think that adoption and foster care is without its rewards and benefits. The biggest thing to keep in mind is that it is about the *children*, not anything else. I do not want to discourage anyone from becoming involved with caring for the needs of these children and perhaps even becoming a forever family for them. But I do believe that everyone needs to go into this with eyes wide open, well prepared for the journey ahead. The reason many of these adoptions and foster placements are failing is a lack of full disclosure, both during the licensing process and then especially with placements. There is such an importance placed on privacy and need to know that there is quite literally no knowing at all.

My attitude is that once children are in need of being removed from a home, all concerns over privacy and need to know should go right out the window. The placement resource has an overriding need to know everything there is about the placement—especially the reasons for removal and what type of behaviors are to be expected. In Clark County, if you are licensed with the county, once a placement is taken, you must give a ten-day notice that you are not willing to take of care of the children anymore. I know of at least one private foster agency that has a thirty-day notice requirement. This helps the system find another resource for the care of the child, but also places the child in danger of not being cared for in the best way possible, as well as creating an unstable environment for the children, leading to even more issues with behavior.

Full disclosure should be a requirement for any placement. Many behaviors can be dealt with if the background of the child is known. If children are coming from abusive homes, certain things can be expected and will not come as a surprise when they surface. The same holds true for alcohol and drug abuse and the most insidious form of abuse there is, sexual. If these issues were known up front, I am convinced that many problems related to foster care could be eliminated. Foster parents would not be blindsided by behavior that is not expected or that was not discussed in the training classes for foster licensing.

I believe that every potential foster parent should have to attend training on *all* types of placements, especially special-needs placements. Most foster placements we have had would definitely be considered special needs—if not medically, then for sure behaviorally. Our adopted children were in a therapeutic foster home until they were placed with us for adoption. My question is why the department would place them with us when we were not considered a therapeutic home and were not prepared for the issues that have surfaced and still are, especially since we were an adoption resource. We were in no way ready or prepared for what surfaced, or for problems that had not been addressed in over three years in the system. This includes medical issues as well as behaviors that manifest in ways sometimes so bizarre they defy description.

Children need to be placed in the correct type of home. If they have special needs, they should be placed in a high-level foster home where the caregivers are trained for the types of behavior they display. This will eliminate a substantial number of failed placements.

Requiring foster parents to give ten days' notice or more is only going to result in more child abuse, neglect, and untimely death. Foster parents shouldn't be chastised for not complying with the full required number of days; instead, they should be commended for having the courage to know that they were doing the right thing in not perpetuating an unhappy or unsafe situation for all concerned.

The foster system must provide services for the placements, including mental-health care and anger-management training. Currently, there are so few providers that this is either lacking or there is a long waiting list. The system is failing the children, and the result is behavioral issues both while the children are in the system and when they return home.

Caseworkers and courts should concentrate on the best interests of the child, instead of trying to reunify with the parent at any cost. When a child is taken into the custody of DFS, a caseworker is assigned to the case. She oversees both the parents and the child. This is a conflict, and I believe the case should be split. One caseworker should be for the child and another for the parents. Judges need to listen to the caseworkers and foster parents before blindly ordering children back to the parents.

It is easy to write and talk about how broken the system is. Everyone knows this and agrees this is the case—even the very people who work in it and administer the programs. The big question is, what can be done to turn this around and correct the shortcomings to prevent tragedies? I've suggested some immediate remedies above, but the most obvious solution would be to correct the social and economic issues that bring about the need for a foster-care system in the first place. This is a monumental task and very sadly will probably never come about. There are many ways that inroads can be made, however. One would be a complete overhaul of the welfare system in general.

It seems as if the system rewards people for having more children and staying at home to have more. For every child who is brought into a household, the amount of aid goes up. This creates an endless cycle that is almost impossible to break. It may sound bigoted, but the mothers of these children have most likely been born into this lifestyle. They only think of how to get the next check and increase the amount, and the fastest and easiest way to do that is to have more kids. What they do not think about is that for every child born, the expenses of caring for that child are added to the mix.

It is a fact of biology that it takes two to make a baby. Therefore, the father should be held accountable for his actions. This is not always possible, as the father is not known or the mother will not give up who he is. So here we go. What to do now?

The first step is education. The second is to change the way welfare is paid. The third is to enforce the guidelines and limit the amount of and length of time aid can be received. The incentives to sit at home and produce more babies have to be taken away. There are many conflicting viewpoints on this, but like the foster-care system, very few, if any, would argue that the system is just fine as it is and does not need reform.

We have seen firsthand the results of the current system and the huge toll it takes on the children who are the innocent victims of their parents' bad decisions. Before we go on, it has to be mentioned that welfare abuse and/or use is not the cause of every case that requires intervention by child-welfare programs, nor is every parent whose children are taken into the system on welfare or a recipient of any other type of aid. The issue is that there is no incentive for those getting a handout to get off these programs and start contributing to society.

The other thing that has to be thought of is that there are only so many dollars that can be spread out over the entire welfare system. If we start to eliminate the fraud and waste from systems that do not work, there will be more money for programs that are needed, such as the foster-care system. Eliminating the incentives for making babies will both reduce the number of affected children who enter the system and reduce the enormous payouts that are not justified. The children are the victims no matter what the cause of their situation is. The idea is to get rid of the situation to begin with. No problem can ever be resolved if the root cause is not corrected.

Education is a subject matter big enough for multiple books. That is another system that is completely broken, and it is the one thing that should be shielded from cutbacks. Money being wasted on welfare could be rechanneled into education and over time produce a huge benefit. Anyone receiving any type of welfare check should be required to attend life-skills and money-management classes. Additionally, welfare recipients should be required to attend vocational and job-skills training, as well as complete a high-school education. This would help eliminate the reward system that is in place now to stay at home and make more babies, with no motivation to get out and work or even look for a job.

There should also be time limits on how long benefits can be received. To many, this will seem harsh, and maybe it is—but so is the way things are now. Every person collecting a check who does not produce any work in exchange is doing nothing but freeloading off the rest of society. We have to be willing to change the way we think and get rid of the mentality that we are owed everything and do not have to work for it. If we start educating citizens to be self-supporting, drop the me-first attitude, and take accountability for their own well-being instead of blaming everyone else for their shortcomings and failures, we would find ourselves in a much more balanced and pleasant society. We need to start taking care of ourselves and not let society bear the costs of what we do not want to do—or more correctly, are too lazy to do.

Once a person who is receiving welfare is in compliance with the education and training requirements, limits must be placed on the length of time these benefits can be received. Six to eight months would not seem unreasonable. That should be sufficient time to find an income with diligent searching. This would be another requirement for receiving aid. If you're not looking for work, you do not get a check.

You may be wondering what all this has to do with the child-welfare system and foster care. These scenarios mentioned above do relate to foster children. If the wastes were stopped and the money channeled as described above, there would be at least two benefits to the foster-care system.

First, the stream of children entering the system would begin to drop. That would start to free up resources spent on the sheer numbers of children entering the system, as they would not need to if their birth families were providing for them. It also would teach much-needed parenting and life skills to those who need it the most so that they can remove themselves from the circular trap of welfare. That again would free up resources to fund education and vocational training. It would also allow for better care of those children who had to enter the system because of incarceration or noncompliance of the parents.

Second, the persons in the welfare program would become productive members of society instead of a drain on resources. That would allow many more children removed from their homes to be placed back there, as the parents would have the life and parenting skills to provide for their children. That would reduce the number of emotionally damaged children being shuffled from home to home with no sense of permanency or belonging. I propose that it would have a very noticeable statistical downward effect on crime rates. It would also reduce the amount of counseling and social services needed to help misplaced children cope with abandonment and neglect. They, in turn, would gain the ability and life skills necessary to become productive citizens themselves.

The welfare system is a monumental problem that is going to require some seismic shifts in thinking. Drastic measures will have to be taken to bring about change and correct the broken mess we have today. It is not a pleasant task to undertake; it will take years to bring about change and make things better for the ones who are affected the most by this— the innocent children. They did not have a choice in being born or what they were born into. It is the responsibility of all of us to see that they are taken care of, regardless of what becomes of their birth parents. Only with the resolve of society at large can we bring about these reforms and stop the endless cycle the current system supports. Only by making some very tough and—in many circles—very unpopular choices can this be reversed and the system corrected.

We must always keep in mind that we are here to protect the children and that they are our future. The generations we raise today are going to be the ones who take care of us. If they care for us the same way we took care of them, we will be in a lot of trouble in our old age.

Giving selflessly to help an innocent child is one of the greatest joys a person can experience. While no one can claim the system is perfect, it is the only resource available to help the true victims here: the children. Only by becoming involved and being an advocate for change and improvement will there be any hope of finding a safe and happy home for children while they go through what has to be the most confusing and frightening period of their lives.

In the resources section at the end of the book, I've listed a variety of web pages for further investigation into both adoption and foster parenting. The Internet is full of information on both how to become a foster parent and how to adopt. There is a vast wealth of knowledge on the problems and issues that have been discussed in this book. I would encourage anyone interested in learning more about fostering and adopting to do their research and go into the process well prepared for what they are signing up for.

About the Author

Janet Solander is a mother of four biological daughters and three adopted young daughters. She works in the medical field as a registered nurse and holds two degrees, including a bachelor's degree in nursing and a bachelor's degree in health-care administration. Janet and her husband are currently fostering a sibling group of four, in addition to caring for their own three adopted daughters.

Janet is in the beginning stages of forming a nonprofit organization to advocate for foster parents and foster children and to address the issues they encounter dealing with the foster-care system, including the lack of proper health care available for these children, especially mental-health-care services. She feels that although there are support groups out there for foster parents, there is not enough support available to address all of the concerns of foster parents. She believes that an advocate's voice is needed specifically for the benefit of the foster parent.

She currently lives in Las Vegas, Nevada, with her husband and three adopted daughters.

Resources

To find out more about the issues I've discussed in this book, consult these online sources:

Foster Care

- "Achieving Stable and Appropriate Placement Settings for Children in Foster Care." *Child Welfare Outcomes 2008–2011: Report to Congress.* US Department of Health and Human Services, Administration for Children and Families. 2009. https://www.acf.hhs.gov/sites/default/files/cb/cwo08_11. pdf#page=41.
- "Characteristics of Foster and Adoptive Families." Washoe County, Nevada, Department of Social Services. http://www. washoecounty.us/socsrv/socsrv_child_fostercare_types_ characteristics.html.
- "State Statutes Search." Child Welfare Information Gateway. 2012–2013. www.childwelfare.gov/systemwide/laws_policies/ state.
- "Foster Care Statistics 2011." Child Welfare Information Gateway. May 2012. https://www.childwelfare.gov/pubs/factsheets/foster. pdf.
- "Trends in Foster Care and Adoption—FY 2002–FY 2012." US Department of Health and Human Services Administration for Children and Families. June 2011. http://www.acf.hhs.gov/sites/ default/files/cb/trends_fostercare_adoption2012.pdf.
- Kendall, M. "Shortage of Foster Parents Seen as U.S. Trend." *USA Today*, September 22, 2010. http://usatoday30.usatoday. com/news/nation/2010-09-23-fostercare23_ST_N.htm.

- "Will New Foster Care Licensing Rules Lose More Foster Homes." Adoption.com, July 16, 2008. http://foster-care.adoptionblogs. com/weblogs/will-new-foster-care-licensing-rules-los.
- "State Gives Most Foster Parents a Raise; but Some See Cuts." *The Oregonian.* http://www.oregonlive.com/politics/index. ssf/2009//10/state_gives_most_foster_parent.html.
- "The High Cost of Foster Care Abuse." *The CPS Racket*, February 2012. http://cpsracket.blogspot.com/2012/02high-cost-of-foster-care-abuse.html.
- Herman, E. "Fostering and Foster Care." The Adoption History Project, February 24, 2012. http://pages.uoregon.edu/adoption/ topics/fostering.htm.

Murder in Foster Care

- Off, G. "Study Puts Blame on DHS For Deaths of Five Children." *Tulsa World*, March 18, 2011. http://www.tulsaworld.com/ article.aspx/Study_puts_blame_on_DHS_for_deaths_of_five_ children/20110318_11_a9_achild667628.
- Mason, Y. "Murdered Children in the Hands of Foster Parents and CPS." *How Child Protective Services Buys and Sells Our Children,* September 12, 2011. http:// protectingourchildrenfrombeingsold.wordpress.com/category/ murdered-children-at-the-hands-of-foster-parents-and-cps/.

Shameeka Davis

- Anthony, L. "Antioch Teen Death Details Released." ABC 7 News, September 4, 2008. http://abclocal.go.com/kgo/ story?section=news/local&id=6371586.
- Hawkins, S. "Starved and Beaten to Death." *Our Weekly*, September 10, 2008. http://ourweekly.com/news/2008/sep/10/ starved-and-beaten-to-death/#.Ujm8ARYmzdk.
- "Trial Begins for Antioch Woman Accused of Niece's Torture, Murder." CBS San Francisco, June 7, 2011. http://sanfrancisco. cbslocal.com/2011/06/07/trial-begins-for-antioch-woman-accused-of-nieces-torture-murder/.

- Fraley, M. "Antioch Foster Mother Sentenced to Life in Prison for Killing Niece, Torturing Nephew." *Contra Costa Times*, January 6, 2012. http://www.mercurynews.com/news/ci_19689187.
- "$4 million settlement for abused foster child in SF." *California's Children*, February 17, 2011. http://californiaschildren.typepad.com/californias-children/2011/02/4-million-settlement-for-abused-foster-child-in-sf.html.

Jorge and Carmen Barahona

- "Florida's Horrific Child Murder." *The Daily Beast*, February 19, 2011. http://www.thedailybeast.com/articles/2011/02/19/jorge-barahona-accused-of-horrific-child-abuse-in-florida.html.

Renée Bowman

- Morse, D. "Mother Convicted of Killing Daughters, Stuffing Them in Freezer." *The Washington Post*, March 22, 2010. http://voices.washingtonpost.com/crime-scene/calvert/mother-convicted-in-freezer-de.html.

Melanie Ochs

- Jourdian, K. "County Commission OKs Settlement in Baby's Death in Foster Care." *Las Vegas Review-Journal*, March 6, 2012. http://www.reviewjournal.com/news/crime-courts/county-commission-oks-settlement-babys-death-foster-care.

Adoption

- "Adoption Disruption and Dissolution." Child Welfare Information Gateway. December 2004. http://www.childwelfare.gov/pubs/s_disrup.cfm.
- "Debunking the Myths: Facts About Foster Care Adoption." National Adoption Day. 2007. http://www.nationaladoptionday.org/media/public/files/media_room/Myths.pdf.

- "State Statutes Search." Child Welfare Information Gateway. 2012–2013. www.childwelfare.gov/systemwide/laws_policies/state.

International

- "Parental Age Limits in International Adoption." *Adoption.com,* April 2, 2007. http://older-parent.adoptionblogs.com/weblogs/parental-age-limits-in-international-ado.
- Keisling, B. "Russian Child Killed in US: Warnings Ignored." *Pravda*, November 3, 2012. http://english.pravda.ru/opinion/feedback/11-03-2010/112540-russian_child_killed-0/.

Child Abuse and Neglect

- "Child Abuse and Neglect Statistics." Child Welfare Information Gateway. 2012. https://www.childwelfare.gov/systemwide/statistics/can.cfm.
- "Child Abuse and Neglect User Manual Series." Child Welfare Information Gateway. 2006. https://www.childwelfare.gov/pubs/usermanual.cfm.
- "State Statutes Search." Child Welfare Information Gateway. 2012–2013. www.childwelfare.gov/systemwide/laws_policies/state.

Child Protective Services

- "Supervising Child Protective Services Caseworkers." Child Welfare Information Gateway. https://www.childwelfare.gov/pubs/usermanuals/supercps/supercpsi.cfm.
- *NASW Standards for Social Work Practice in Child Welfare.* National Association of Social Workers. 2005. http://www.socialworkers.org/practice/standards/childwelfarestandards2012.pdf.
- "Class Action Lawsuit against CPS/DPSS/DFS/HRS." Care2 Petition Site. http://www.thepetitionsite.com/3/class-action-lawsuit-against-cpsdpsdfshrs-for-kidnapping-babies-to-sell.

Mental-Health Issues

- Salahi, L., and J. Diaz. "Antipsychotics for Foster Kids: Most Commonly Prescribed Meds." ABC News, December 1, 2011. http://abcnews.go.com/Health/Wellness/foster-children-commonly-prescribed-antipsychotics/story?id=15056937.
- "State Attorney General Sues Drug Company." *Austin American-Statesman*. http://www.statesman.com/news/news/state-regional/state-attorney-general-sues-drug-company-1/nRjZR/.
- "Eating Problems in Foster Children." *Neglect: The Hole in the Middle* (web-based course). The Alaska Center for Resource Families. http://www.acrf.org/Self-StudyCourses/neglectcourse/n2eating.htm.